GARDENING WITH
SHRUBS

GARDENING WITH SHRUBS

ERIC SAWFORD

**GUILD OF MASTER CRAFTSMAN
PUBLICATIONS LTD**

First published 2003 by
Guild of Master Craftsman Publications Ltd,
166 High Street, Lewes,
East Sussex, BN7 1XN

Text © Eric Sawford 2003
© in the work GMC Publications Ltd

ISBN 1 86108 306 8

All rights reserved

The right of Eric Sawford to be identified as the author of this work has been asserted in accordance with the Copyright Designs and Patents Act 1988, Sections 77 and 78.

No part of this publication may be reproduced, stored in a retrieval system, or transmitted in any form or by any means without the prior permission of the publisher and copyright owner.

This book is sold subject to the condition that all designs are copyright and are not for commercial reproduction without the written permission of the designer and copyright owner.

The publishers and authors can accept no legal responsibility for any consequences arising from the application of information, advice or instructions given in this publication.

British Cataloguing in Publication Data
A catalogue record of this book is available from the British Library.

Edited by Graham Clarke
Designed by Andy Harrison
All photographs by Eric Sawford
Illustrations by John Yates

Typeface: Gill Sans

Colour origination by Universal Graphics, Singapore

Printed and bound in Hong Kong by CT Printing Ltd

To Noreen with much love,
and thanks for her endless help in the preparation of this book

CONTENTS

CHAPTER ONE
Introduction — 1

CHAPTER TWO
The Flowering Year — 8

CHAPTER THREE
Soil and Planting — 18

CHAPTER FOUR
Care and Maintenance — 28

CHAPTER FIVE
Propagation — 36

CHAPTER SIX
Shrub Troubles — 44

CHAPTER SEVEN
Plant Directory — 52

CHAPTER EIGHT
Handy Guides — 150

CHAPTER NINE
Glossary — 156

About the author — 161

Index — 162

LEFT *Acer palmatum* 'Bloodgood' is well known for its richly coloured foliage that turns red in the autumn

CHAPTER ONE

INTRODUCTION

LEFT The apothecary's rose (*Rosa gallica officinalis*)

GARDENING WITH **SHRUBS**

INTRODUCTION

Shrubs have a very important part to play in any well-planned garden – not only for providing a long-term background for numerous other plants, but also for their display of flowers and, in some cases, attractive foliage and fruits. The old idea of confining shrubs to their own border has long since gone.

It is possible to have shrubs in flower throughout the year, even in the depths of winter, when blooms are particularly welcome to brighten up the garden at an otherwise dismal time. The flowers of some shrubs are fragrant, and some are attractive to wildlife – the one most liked by butterflies and bees is buddleja, well known by its common name of 'butterfly bush'. Shrubs can also be used to provide a windbreak, or as a screen for privacy.

The choice available is enormous. Not so long ago they were usually sold as 'bare-root' or, in the case of evergreens, with their roots 'balled' (this is where the soil and roots are left intact, and tightly wrapped with sacking). In both cases planting was restricted to the autumn or early spring. Today, most shrubs are container-grown. This has the advantage that they can be planted

LEFT *Rhododendron* **'Golden Flare' carries large attractive blooms in early summer**

GARDENING WITH SHRUBS

ABOVE **A 'balled' shrub. The roots are wrapped tightly in sacking or similar material**

ABOVE **A container-grown shrub. Carefully tease apart the bottom roots before planting**

ABOVE **Pre-packed shrubs are stored in a plastic bag within a carton. There may be some peat present**

at any time other than in frosty, very wet or extremely dry conditions.

Container-grown plants are available from garden centres and nurserymen. Many large garden centres, however, limit their range to the more popular kinds. Nurserymen who specialize in shrubs will stock the well-known favourites, but also rare subjects that are seldom seen for sale.

Shrubs are also sold pre-packed, which can be seen in retail outlets such as supermarkets. These are bare-rooted stock plants, the roots of which are surrounded by moist peat; it is certainly a cheaper way of buying them. Care must be taken with these, as warm conditions in shops can lead to the plants putting on growth prematurely. These should also be planted in suitable conditions outdoors, from autumn through to spring.

When you buy plants do not be misled by colourful labels; take time to check whether a

INTRODUCTION

particular subject is suitable for you. There are many important points to consider.

First, there is the question of soil type. While many shrubs will grow in a wide range of conditions, others require a soil that has a greater acidic value. If you live in an alkaline (chalky soil) area and wish to grow subjects such as rhododendrons, choose compact varieties, plant them in a container of ericaceous compost (suitable for acid-loving plants), and water them with collected rainwater.

Then there is the eventual size of the plant; there is nothing worse than finding that something is planted in the wrong place because it has rapidly outgrown its allocated area, and you have to cut it back or dig it out.

Also there you should consider the 'hardiness' of the shrub. It is always advisable to study the label and, if necessary, ask advice or look it up in an appropriate reference book before making your purchase.

There are numerous dwarf shrubs that are splendid subjects for the rock garden. These will vary in height and variety. Allow plenty of space so that they can be left undisturbed to grow into attractive specimen plants.

Shrubs have many other attributes, too. Colourful berries, fascinating stems and ornamental bark are found on many. Some are at their best in the depths of winter, and among these are the dogwoods. One that certainly catches the eye on a bright winter's day is *Cornus stolonifera* 'Sibirica' with its glowing red stems; it looks wonderful when accompanied by at least one of the winter-flowering heathers. By way of contrast, do not overlook the green-stemmed *C. alba* 'Flaviramea', or the ornamental brambles that are grown for their silver-white branches. One of the best is *Rubus cockburnianus*.

The rose is very well known among shrubs, ranging from the neat, compact hybrid teas, to the free-flowering floribundas and the increasingly popular forms of 'English rose'. These are just three of the groups available: there are legions of varieties with a constant supply of newcomers swelling the ranks.

Those whose gardens are on acid soil can grow some of the most flamboyant shrubs of all – the *Rhododendron*, with its trusses of brilliantly

ABOVE *Cornus stolonifera* 'Sibirica' – a first-class shrub for winter colour

GARDENING WITH **SHRUBS**

coloured or pastel blooms (these now include shrubs that at one time were listed as azaleas). There are numerous other shrubs that require similar soil conditions, such as forms of *Pieris* with their bright red young foliage, followed by loose sprays of bell-shaped 'lily of the valley' like blooms. A shrub that is not as popular as it deserves is *Corylopsis;* this produces tiny tassels of fragrant yellow flowers before the foliage. Its position should be chosen with care; a lightly shaded and sheltered spot is required as the blooms can be damaged by frost.

Among the most useful subjects for a winter garden are the heathers. Many flower in the depths of winter and are seemingly unaffected by all that the weather can throw at them. Look out for those in the *Erica carnea* and *Erica × darleyensis* groups. Both are lime-tolerant, which makes them ideal for a wide variety of gardens.

LEFT 'Mama Mia' – a splendid rhododendron in the azalea group; one of the many whites

ABOVE *Rubus cockburnianus* **'Golden Vale' carries lovely golden foliage in summer and white shoots in winter**

INTRODUCTION

ABOVE *Erica carnea* 'King George' – the carnea group of heathers will grow in chalky soils

Erica carnea grows to around 25cm (10in) and flowers from early winter through to spring. Making a choice is not easy as there are so many. Two well-known and proven forms are 'Springwood White' and the deep red 'Vivellii'.

Varieties of *E.* × *darleyensis* start to bloom in mid-autumn and also go on through the most difficult time of the year. They grow taller, in most cases reaching 45cm (18in). Look for 'Darley Dale', a rich pink, and 'Molton Silver' with white flowers. By choosing carefully it is possible to have heathers in bloom throughout the year.

Each year gardeners are introduced to a new array of shrubs; do not be afraid to try any you fancy. In order to avoid disappointment, always remember the basic rules: check soil type, and check on the eventual height and spread (before buying), and follow the planting procedures. Thereafter, furnishing your garden with healthy shrubs dripping with colourful flowers or berries, is as easy as ABC.

A note about seasons

For the benefit of readers in both hemispheres, seasons – rather than months – are referred to throughout this book. The following table shows the approximate month for each season:

NORTHERN HEMISPHERE				SOUTHERN HEMISPHERE
Early winter	=	**January**	=	Early summer
Mid-winter	=	**February**	=	Mid-summer
Late winter	=	**March**	=	Late summer
Early spring	=	**April**	=	Early autumn
Mid-spring	=	**May**	=	Mid-autumn
Late spring	=	**June**	=	Late autumn
Early summer	=	**July**	=	Early winter
Mid-summer	=	**August**	=	Mid-winter
Late summer	=	**September**	=	Late winter
Early autumn	=	**October**	=	Early spring
Mid-autumn	=	**November**	=	Mid-spring
Late autumn	=	**December**	=	Late spring

CHAPTER TWO

THE **FLOWERING** YEAR

LEFT *Hydrangea macrophylla* is at its best in mid-summer

GARDENING WITH **SHRUBS**

THE FLOWERING YEAR

With careful selection it is possible to have shrubs in flower during every month of the year. Given below are some suggestions.

Early winter

Erica carnea
Erica × darleyensis
Garrya elliptica
Hamamelis (all forms)
Jasminum nudiflorum
Lonicera fragrantissima
Viburnum × bodnantense
Viburnum tinus

Mid-winter

Abeliophyllum
Daphne mezereum
Daphne odora
Erica (as mentioned above)
Hamamelis japonica
Mahonia 'Charity'

Late winter

Camellia japonica
Chaenomeles
Cornus mas
Corylopsis
Forsythia
Mahonia
Ribes
Salix
Spiraea (some)

LEFT *Cornus controversa* 'Variegata', often referred to as the wedding cake tree

GARDENING WITH SHRUBS

THE FLOWERING YEAR

Early spring

Berberis (several)
Clematis alpina
Kerria japonica
Magnolia × *soulangiana*
Osmanthus delavayi
Rosmarinus officinalis
Skimmia
Spiraea
Viburnum (spring flowering)

Mid-spring

Choisya ternata
Clematis
Cotoneaster
Crinodendron hookerianum
Cytisus
Daphne (some)
Genista
Pyracantha
Rhododendron

Late spring

Buddleja
Cistus
Clematis
Convolvulus cneorum
Deutzia
Genista
Kalmia latiflora
Syringa
Weigela

LEFT **Rhododendron luteum – a very fragrant shrub in the Azalea Group**

GARDENING WITH **SHRUBS**

THE FLOWERING YEAR

Early summer

Calluna vulgaris
Erica (summer flowering)
Hypericum
Lavandula
Lavatera
Potentilla
Spiraea

Mid-summer

Ceanothus (late-flowering varieties)
Ceratostigma willmottianum
Fuchsia
Hibiscus syriacus
Hydrangea
Perovskia
Yucca

Late summer

Abelia grandiflora
Erica
Fuchsia
Hebe
Hibiscus
Hydrangea
Hypericum
Osmanthus heterophyllus
Potentilla (many)
Yucca gloriosa
Zauschneria

LEFT **French lavender (*Lavandula stoechas*) requires a warm spot, in well-drained soil**

GARDENING WITH **SHRUBS**

THE FLOWERING YEAR

Early autumn

Abelia
Calluna
Erica
Fuchsia
Hebe (some)
Hibiscus
Hypericum 'Hidcote'

Mid-autumn

Erica x *darleyensis*
Jasminum nudiflorum
Viburnum x *bodnantense*

Late autumn

Camellia x *williamsii*
Hamamelis mollis
Jasminum nudiflorum
Mahonia x *media*
Viburnum x *bodnantense*
Viburnum tinus

LEFT Witch hazels flower in the coldest months. This is *Hamamelis mollis* **'Pagoda'**

CHAPTER THREE

SOIL AND **PLANTING**

LEFT *Rhododendron* Bluebird Group: compact, early flowering shrubs

GARDENING WITH SHRUBS

SOIL AND PLANTING

The vast majority of shrubs are happy in good humus-rich, well-drained soil. Avoid any locations that are badly drained or, even worse, waterlogged during the winter months. As with all rules there are exceptions, and principal among these are the 'lime-haters', that is, the plants that only thrive if grown in soil that is more acidic than alkaline.

Before deciding on what to plant it is a good idea to have the soil analysed. This will not only tell you if the conditions are alkaline, but also if there are any trace elements that are absent.

Among the plants that will not tolerate lime are forms of *Camellia*, *Pieris* and *Rhododendron*. These require acid soil conditions, ideally enriched with leaf mould.

The first thing to consider is how your shrub has been supplied. Those grown in containers can be planted at any time of the year, provided that soil conditions are suitable. It is best to avoid times when the ground is frozen or very wet, or if it is very dry and the weather is hot generally.

Prior to the widespread use of containers, shrubs were supplied bare-rooted during the

LEFT *Berberis* x *stenophylla* 'Corallina Compacta' is one of the best of the low-growing barberries

ABOVE *Daphne cneorum* **'Eximia'** – a prostrate form of this free-flowering shrub

dormant season; even today some still are. Here, the planting period should be between early autumn and late winter. The same applies for pre-packed shrubs sold in numerous retail outlets. Examine these carefully: if the roots are dry, plunge them in water for an hour or so before planting out.

Another method used by nurserymen is to supply evergreen shrubs 'balled'. These shrubs have been dug up and the rootballs tightly wrapped with sacking or other protective material. It is important that the roots do not dry out during the period that the plants are wrapped and stored. They should not, therefore, come to any harm for several weeks until the soil conditions are suitable. Rhododendrons are often supplied like this.

When purchasing young shrubs it is difficult to appreciate how much space they will eventually need when they're mature. There is a temptation to plant them too closely, eventually resulting in overcrowding and poor or misshapen growth due

SOIL AND PLANTING

ABOVE *Pieris japonica* 'Valley Rose' – deep pink buds fade to white as they open

GARDENING WITH **SHRUBS**

ABOVE *Pittosporum tenuifolium* 'Gold Star'

SOIL AND PLANTING

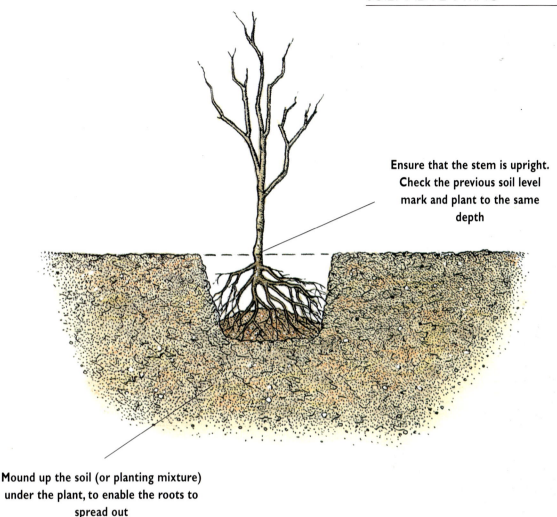

Ensure that the stem is upright. Check the previous soil level mark and plant to the same depth

Mound up the soil (or planting mixture) under the plant, to enable the roots to spread out

ABOVE **Cross-section of a bare-rooted shrub at planting time**

to lack of light. If you wish to fill a space quickly or temporarily, rather than choose and plant an inappropriate shrub you should perhaps consider a herbaceous perennial, or even an inexpensive shrub alternative. This can be removed at a later stage, when the priority shrubs have made sufficient growth.

Planting

Most container stock is grown in peat-based compost, which can sometimes lead to problems when planting out. The roots suddenly find themselves trying to grow in less hospitable garden soil. This shock to their system can be minimized by using a planting mixture obtained from garden centres, or a home-made concoction of topsoil, peat and a little bonemeal fertilizer, all mixed well.

If, when you remove the plant from its container, you see that the roots are pot-bound, gently tease them apart at the bottom. This will encourage them to establish more quickly.

The planting hole should be larger and deeper than required. Spread a 10cm (4in) layer of the planting mixture in the bottom of the hole and place the shrub over it. There should be enough space in the hole for some of the mixture to be placed around the sides as well. The surface of the surrounding soil should be just slightly raised from the compost level of the shrub, so that water will collect in the 'well' that

GARDENING WITH **SHRUBS**

ABOVE *Salix integra* 'Hikuro-Nishiki' is good for waterside planting in a lightly shaded spot

Ensure that the plant is planted at the correct depth. The top of the 'rootball' should be level with the surrounding soil

The hole should be large enough to add a 10cm (4in) layer of planting mixture at the base and around the sides of the rootball

ABOVE Cross-section of a container-grown shrub at planting time

SOIL AND PLANTING

Create a shallow reservoir around the base of the shrub, in order to prevent water from running away before it soaks in

Really soak newly planted shrubs – with a hosepipe or watering can. Do not simply 'dribble' a little water on to them

ABOVE **A regular supply of water is crucial to newly planted shrubs, especially in hot, dry weather**

has been created. This will help to prevent drying out in hot weather.

Firm well around the roots to increase their contact with the soil, and to lose any air pockets, which will cause roots to dry out.

A similar planting procedure is used with balled plants, pre-packaged and bare-root stock. Here again, dig a hole large enough for the roots to be spread out. Work the planting mixture well around the roots, and firm as you go. Tread the soil gently to firm. It is important that the old soil mark on the stem is just below the soil level when planting is finished. Water well.

It is advisable to cut back the branches on bare-rooted shrubs by one third, to help speed their establishment in the soil. Plants purchased in containers do not need this treatment.

Cold winds and severe weather can cause damage to the foliage of some evergreen shrubs when planted in the autumn. This can be avoided by erecting a shelter of polythene sheeting around any that are liable to be damaged. Secure it well, to avoid it being blown away in high winds, and ensure the base is fixed down to avoid draughts.

CHAPTER FOUR

CARE AND
MAINTENANCE

LEFT *Prunus incisa* 'Kojo-no-mai' is slow-growing, and a good shrub for a container

GARDENING WITH **SHRUBS**

CARE AND MAINTENANCE

Having completed the planting, the next thing to consider is the provision of support for any shrubs with weak or lax branches. This will encourage roots to establish and become an anchor for the plant, especially in the case of tall subjects.

Mulching will help to conserve moisture and suppress the growth of weeds. Hoe carefully to keep down any that do appear, but don't get too close to the plant, or too deep; this could damage any shallow roots. It is better to hand-weed near the plant itself. Renew the mulch annually.

Evergreen shrubs can be damaged by heavy falls of snow. If this is forecast the branches of valuable specimens can be tied with soft twine. After a downfall, shaking them to remove most of the snow should prevent the shrub from coming to any harm. Newly planted specimens of many shrubs will benefit from some form of winter protection.

Dead-heading – removing the faded flowers – has a number of advantages. Not only does it keep the shrub tidy, it can, in some cases, often result in a further flush of flowers later in the year. Dead-heading also prevents seed formation.

LEFT *Hebe ochracea* **'James Stirling' seldom flowers; it is grown principally for its foliage**

GARDENING WITH **SHRUBS**

ABOVE Mulching around the base of shrubs, with pulverized bark, peat, or well-rotted compost or manure, will help to retain moisture in the soil and keep down weed growth

There are a few instances where the flowers should be left until the following spring. Among these are hydrangeas, where the dead flowers help to protect the following year's growth buds throughout the winter.

Take care when removing the dead flowers of rhododendrons: snap them off with your finger and thumb, as it is easy to damage new growth.

Watering

This is extremely important with newly planted shrubs. Always water copiously, as a light sprinkling can do more harm than good, by encouraging roots to the surface of the soil. Plants on light soils will dry out quickly, so regular watering will be necessary in prolonged spells of dry weather. When the shrubs are well established, watering will not be required so often, especially if a mulch is used. One method to ensure new stock is well watered is to build a ridge of soil around each shrub and fill the resultant basin with water.

This is particularly useful in the case of shrubs with shallow roots, such as rhododendrons, which can suffer quickly in periods of drought.

Pruning

This is important to produce healthy, vigorous plants of good shape, and at the same time will remove any stray, unwanted or weak, dead or diseased branches. This work should be carried out at different times throughout the year, depending on the subject (see appropriate plant section).

While there are exceptions, as a rough guide deciduous shrubs that flower early in the year are

CARE AND MAINTENANCE

ABOVE *Aucuba japonica* 'Variegata' berries only appear on the female varieties

ABOVE *Pyracantha* 'Orange Glow' – masses of berries, not liked by birds

CARE AND MAINTENANCE

normally cut back immediately after flowering, and any unwanted branches removed.

Deciduous shrubs that flower in the summer and autumn are generally pruned before growth starts in the early spring. There are exceptions, however. The mock oranges (*Philadelphus*), for example, flower on wood produced the previous year. They should, therefore, receive attention immediately after flowering.

Evergreen shrubs are normally pruned (if necessary) in mid-spring.

In all cases you should prune back to healthy wood. All cuts must be clean, with a sloping cut just above an outward-facing bud. Collect up all prunings, and burn any that are diseased.

Invest in a good pair of two-bladed secateurs. For larger shrubs long-handled pruners are essential. Make sure any tools used are sharp and kept clean.

Feeding

Many shrubs will benefit from a mulch of well-rotted compost or manure applied in late autumn or during the winter. As they grow they take valuable nutrients from the soil, so a light sprinkling of a well-balanced fertilizer lightly raked in is beneficial during the spring. Foliar feeding can also occasionally be used, but you should cease all feeding from late summer.

ABOVE *Pittosporum tenuifolium* '**Purpureum**' is a large shrub; pale green leaves turn to bronze-purple

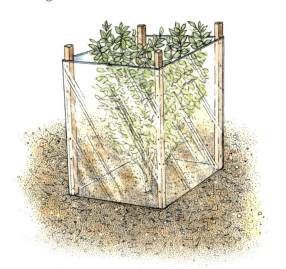

ABOVE Some shrubs are slightly tender when young, so would benefit from protection from the worst weather for the first two winters. Screens made from plastic sheeting will help to minimize wind damage

CHAPTER FIVE

PROPAGATION

LEFT *Camellia* 'Adolphe Audusson' – one of the best, with semi-double red flowers

GARDENING WITH **SHRUBS**

PROPAGATION

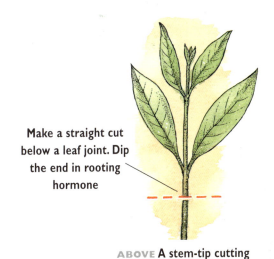

Make a straight cut below a leaf joint. Dip the end in rooting hormone

ABOVE A stem-tip cutting

There are a number of methods of increasing your stock of shrubs. The most common way is from cuttings, and there are basically three types: softwood, heel and hardwood. See the directory section for individual recommendations.

Cuttings

Softwood cuttings These are taken from the tips of the shoots, and should be from 2.5–15cm (1–6in) in length, depending on the plant. Trim each cutting to leave a straight, clean cut below a leaf joint, and take off leaves from the bottom half. Dip the base of the cutting in hormone rooting powder and tap it lightly to remove any surplus. This method is also used for basal cuttings (these are shoots coming from the base of the plant, and are gently pulled away).

Heel cuttings This is the most often used method of increasing shrubs. They are taken from semi-ripe material, i.e. green at the top and woody where it joins the main stem. The method of taking these is to gently pull the chosen cutting material down. It will come away with a small

LEFT *Potentilla fruticosa* 'Limelight' has a long flowering period

39

GARDENING WITH SHRUBS

ABOVE A 'heel' cutting. Pull the shoot away from the main stem, leaving a heel attached

ABOVE A hardwood cutting should be 20–30cm (9–12in) long, depending on the plant

'heel' of outer bark attached. Trim the cutting, leaving some of the heel, and dip it in hormone powder as before.

In both cases it is important to prepare the compost well. It should be of an equal mix of sharp sand and peat. Fill a pot with the compost, making a hole for each cutting with a small dibber. Insert each one, ensuring no air spaces are left (firming the cutting in place, with your fingers or a pencil, will ensure this). Water gently and place them in a closed garden frame. Shade from hot sunshine and ventilate well during the day. Cover the frame if the weather turns frosty. When well rooted, the cuttings can be potted individually to grow on. Alternatively, plant them out into a nursery bed. They are ready to go into their permanent position in the autumn or following spring.

Hardwood cuttings This method is used on a number of shrubs. It is a longer process and normally takes a year or more before the young stock is ready for planting out. Cuttings from well-ripened shoots of the current year's growth are taken in late autumn. They should be 20–30cm (9–12in) long when trimmed. The top should be prepared with a sloping cut immediately above a bud. The base should have a straight cut immediately below a bud.

Dip the base in hormone rooting powder. Select a well-drained, lightly shaded part of the garden and with a spade, take out a small trench with one edge vertical. The bottom of the trench should have a 2.5cm (1in) layer of equal parts course sand/peat mix, to provide a good medium for the roots to grow into. Lay the cuttings around 15cm (6in) apart, against the straight side, and gradually fill and firm the soil as you go. When finished, a third of the cutting should be above soil level.

Heavy winter frost can loosen the soil, so you may need to firm them again. It is essential to keep them watered in dry weather. In around 12 months the cuttings should have rooted sufficiently to plant them into their permanent

PROPAGATION

ABOVE Many shrubs can be propagated by layering. Healthy, flexible shoots are brought into contact with the soil

positions. Hardwood cuttings can also be inserted into a suitably prepared garden frame.

Layering Many shrubs can be increased by layering. Select a young healthy shoot from the plant, and it should be flexible as well, as it needs to be bent over and down to the soil level. With a trowel, take out a small piece of soil where you wish it to root. Place a small amount of sharp sand and peat, in equal amount, into the base of this hole.

Then, make a 2.5cm (1in) long sloping cut on the bottom side of the stem, but take care not to cut through completely and sever it. A matchstick should be placed in the cut to keep it open. Bend the stem down so that the cut area is pushed into the compost mix, and then peg it in place. Cover the area with more of the rooting mixture. Tie the end of the cutting that is above ground level to a small support, to stop it from moving in the wind, or springing back into its normal position. Rooting can take anything from nine months to two years, depending on the type of plant.

Division Some shrubs can be increased by division. This should be done in early winter when soil conditions are suitable. Look out for suckers; these are shoots arising from below the soil surface and from around the base of the plant. Remove these by cutting or pulling from the parent plant, and replant them immediately. Plant them into a similar rooting mixture as described above.

GARDENING WITH **SHRUBS**

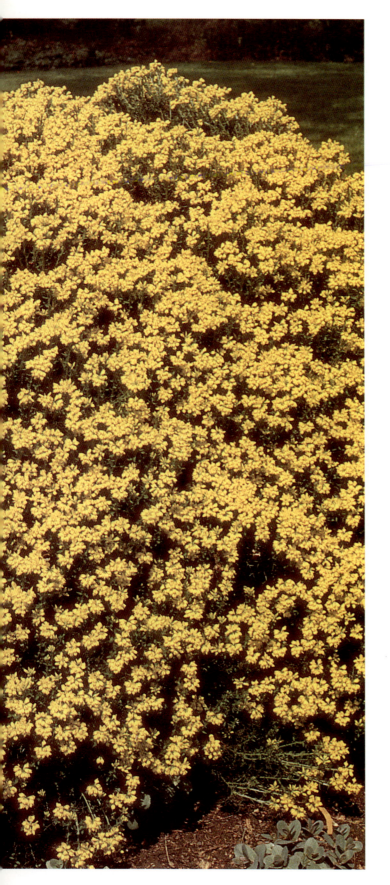

ABOVE *Cistus purpureus* produces a long succession of flowers

LEFT *Genista* – a free-flowering compact shrub

PROPAGATION

Seed Only a few subjects can be raised successfully from seed. Many have problems with germination and can take some time. It is worth considering, however, particularly with forms of *Cistus* and *Genista*. Seed sowing is usually carried out in the spring. Fill a pot with a good loam-based seed compost, firm gently and water, leave to drain. Sow the seed thinly. Space the seed out by hand if they are large enough to handle. Cover larger seeds with a thin layer of compost; fine seed should be left uncovered. Place a polythene bag over the top of the pot, and hold in place with an elastic band. Put the pot into a garden frame and shade it from strong sunlight. When the seedlings are large enough, prick them out individually into 7cm (3in) pots. Repot them into larger pots as required, until they are ready to plant out in the autumn or following spring.

CHAPTER SIX

SHRUB **TROUBLES**

LEFT *Choisya* 'Aztec Pearl', a free-flowering evergreen shrub

GARDENING WITH **SHRUBS**

SHRUB TROUBLES

Sadly it is just not possible to grow a range of shrubs without encountering a few problems along the way. The most common of these are pests and diseases, many of which are instantly recognisable. Fortunately, in most cases, remedies are available – and successful.

Pests

There are a number of pests that will attack shrubs.

■ **Aphids** (greenfly and blackfly) cause discoloration of the leaves and distorted shoots; they also leave a sticky substance known as honeydew. They should be controlled with a systemic insecticide as soon as they are seen, as large colonies can quickly build up.

■ **Vine weevils** are a particularly serious problem. The grubs attack the roots below soil level. Modern biological control is available with the use of nematodes applied to the soil. This must be done when the grubs are active and the soil temperature is right, generally in spring and early autumn. Shrubs most susceptible include *Camellia*, *Clematis* and *Rhododendron*.

LEFT *Rhododendron* 'Irohayama' – a hybrid evergreen azalea

GARDENING WITH **SHRUBS**

ABOVE *Camellia x williamsii* 'Taylor's Perfection': as with all camellias protect from early morning sun after frost

The adult weevils cut small 'U'-shaped holes in the leaf edges, feeding after dark. Spraying shrubs and soil with a systemic insecticide is helpful, or alternatively check after dark and destroy any adults that are found.

■ **Caterpillars** should be treated as soon as seen, as they can seriously damage foliage. Spray with a persistent insecticide.

■ **Birds** can also damage shrubs, especially early in the season, removing flowers from *Forsythia* and *Prunus*.

■ **Red spider mite** is a very serious pest under glass, which can also attack outside, especially in dry conditions. Usual signs include a 'bronzing' of the leaves. Check the undersides of the leaves. If you see a fine webbing of silky hairs and tiny spider-like mites, you'll know that your plant has been attacked. Spray with a suitable insecticide and repeat one month later.

■ Another pest that can sometimes be seen on shrubs is **woolly aphid**, which is indicated by a white waxy wool substance. Brush off and spray with insecticide.

■ Other pests that damage foliage include **capsid bugs** and **chafer beetle**. Spraying foliage and surrounding soil with a systemic insecticide will help to control them.

Diseases

There are a number of fungal diseases that can attack shrubs.

■ **Honey fungus** – a white fungal growth appears below the bark at ground level, and black thread-like rhizomorphs grow through and over the roots. These can travel through the soil and attack other subjects, particularly if they are under stress or damaged. Honey-coloured toadstools appear in the autumn.

There is no cure for the disease, although chemical products are available to treat the soil. Remove all traces of wood, including trunk and roots. Rhododendrons, cherries, lilac and willows are particularly susceptible to this disease.

■ **Canker** will kill any branch it affects. When seen, you should cut it back to clean wood.

■ **Fireblight** will cause the shoots of some shrubs and trees – members of the rose family – to wilt and die. The brown, withered leaves that

ABOVE *Clematis* 'Blue Dancer' is one of the Alpina Group

GARDENING WITH **SHRUBS**

remain on the plant identify this. Cut out and burn the affected branch.

- **Coral spot disease** is easily identifiable with its raised pink spots. Here again, cut out all diseased wood and burn it.
- **Powdery mildew** is a common garden problem. When seen, spray immediately with a systemic fungicide and repeat one week later.

Viruses

Virus diseases can occur on a few shrubs. Insects, tools, or even your hands are known to carry or transmit them, from one subject to another. Always buy clean plant stock. Avoid any that look doubtful, with yellow blotched or crinkly leaves and stunted growth. There is no cure for viruses. Remove the virused plants, or parts of plants, and burn the cuttings. Keep all tools clean, especially secateurs and pruners.

Chlorosis

One problem that can occur on acid-loving shrubs if they are grown where lime is present in the soil, is chlorosis. This is a lime-induced disorder. Leaves become yellow. Treat the plant with a sequestered compound – depending on the severity of the problem, this may cure it.

Nutrient deficiencies

If the soil lacks certain plant nutrients, this will normally show in a change of leaf colour. The leaves themselves will usually indicate what is missing, for example a lack of nitrogen would cause reddish and yellow tints. Leaf-edge scorch can indicate a potash shortage. Magnesium shortage produces a browning between the veins. Iron deficiency causes yellow leaves. The last two can be improved by watering with a sequestered compound, and foliar feeding in the first two cases.

In spring, sprinkle the soil with a good balanced fertilizer and rake it in.

RIGHT *Prunus cerasifera 'Pissardii' flowers early, and will eventually grow into a tree*

CHAPTER SEVEN

PLANT **DIRECTORY**

LEFT *Rhododendron* 'Gibraltar'

GARDENING WITH **SHRUBS**

PLANT DIRECTORY

1. ACER

Common name Maple
Family Aceraceae

There are around 150 species within this family, including deciduous trees and shrubs. They are grown principally for their very attractive foliage, with many leaf forms and colours. Some also have attractive bark. One of the best known is the Japanese maple (*Acer palmatum*), and a number of these are very colourful in the autumn.

Popular species and varieties

Among the taller-growing varieties of *A. palmatum* is 'Bloodgood' (AGM), with lobed dark red-purple foliage that turns bright red in the autumn. Mature specimens can reach 5m (16ft) or more in height. Also taking on good autumn colour is 'Osakazuki' (AGM), which can reach 6m (20ft) in ideal conditions. By contrast, 'Sang-kako' (AGM) produces attractive orange-yellow leaves that, as autumn approaches, turn to a soft yellow before falling. This also grows to around 6m (20ft) in height.

Those in the Dissectum Group of *A. palmatum* have a shrubby habit. They eventually grow into dense, medium-sized bushes and are noted for their finely divided foliage. 'Viride' has bright green leaves, and 'Atropurpureum' has bronze-red foliage. 'Garnet' (AGM) is a good choice with reddish-purple leaves. There are a number of other excellent named varieties, and all of the members of this group are more suitable for smaller gardens.

Cultivation

Soil type Most well-drained soils.
Planting This should be carried out between early autumn and late winter when soil conditions are suitable – not when very wet or frosty. Choose an open sunny or partially shaded spot sheltered from strong winds, as these can damage young foliage in spring and spoil those noted for their autumn colour.
Maintenance No trimming or pruning is required. Clear fallen leaves in the autumn.
Propagation Species can be grown from seed sown in early autumn and placed in a cold frame. Professional nurserymen propagate named varieties by grafting in early spring on to rootstocks of the type species.
Pests and diseases There are a number of problems that can affect acers. An appropriate insecticide can control aphids, scale insects and caterpillars. Tar spot can sometimes affect acers. This produces black blotches with a yellow edge on the leaves during the summer. Collect and destroy any fallen leaves and spray the acer with fungicide.

LEFT *Acer palmatum* 'Dissectum' enjoying cool moist conditions at the edge of a pond

GARDENING WITH SHRUBS

ABOVE *Aucuba japonica* 'Variegata': easily grown in most garden soils

2. AUCUBA

Common name **Laurel**
Family name **Aucubaceae**

The *Aucuba* originates from the Himalayas and parts of East Asia and is among the easiest of all evergreen, hardy shrubs to grow. It will tolerate shady spots, stand up well to atmospheric pollution and salt-laden winds, and has a number of uses in the garden in a spot where little else will flourish. Aucubas make excellent hedges and screens.

Popular species and varieties

Those with variegated foliage, known as the spotted laurels, are the species widely available, together with numerous named forms. *Aucuba japonica* has shiny dark green leaves up to 17cm (8in) in length, and the plant forms a neat, rounded bush. The insignificant flowers appear in late winter and early spring. Plants of both sexes need to be planted in close proximity to produce berries. These are bright red and appear on female plants in early autumn, remaining throughout the winter. There are a considerable number of varieties: 'Crotonifolia' (AGM), a female aucuba with attractive yellow leaves; 'Gold Dust' (female) has foliage heavily speckled golden yellow; 'Variegata' (female) is another good choice. The best male varieties include 'Crassifolia', 'Golden King' and 'Lance Leaf'.

Cultivation

Soil type These easy going shrubs are happy in most types of garden soil, with the exception of waterlogged conditions.
Planting They are not fussy as to location, being successful in sun, dappled or deep shade. Those with variegated foliage are best in light shade.
Maintenance Pruning is not necessary. If grown as a hedge, any trimming required should be done in mid-spring.
Propagation The easiest method of raising new plants is from semi-ripe cuttings taken in the early autumn.
Pests and diseases Generally trouble free.

3. AZARA

Common name none
Family Flacourtiaceae

These evergreen shrubs originate from South America. There are several species available, and they are best grown in a sheltered spot.

Popular species and varieties

Among those offered is *Azara integrifolia* which has an upright habit and can grow to around 5m (16ft) in ideal conditions. The foliage is small, glossy and dark green. In mid-winter the clusters of fragrant yellow flowers start to appear.

A. microphylla (AGM) is regarded as being the hardiest, and is ideal when grown against a wall where it can easily reach to 6m (20ft) or more. It will also grow successfully in shaded areas. The clusters of flowers appear in late winter and are vanilla-scented. There is also a golden variegated form of this species.

A. serrata has toothed, oval leaves, and it flowers in mid-summer. The fragrant dark yellow blooms are held in umbels and are followed by small white berries. A mature specimen of this species can usually reach up to 4m (12ft).

Cultivation

Soil type Most humus-rich, well-drained soils are suitable.
Planting This should be done in the early autumn or spring. Choose a position in partial or light shade.
Maintenance Pruning is not generally required. If necessary, any light trimming back should be done in late winter.
Propagation Semi-ripe cuttings can be taken in late summer.
Pests and diseases In ideal situations they are generally trouble free.

RIGHT **The summer-flowering *Azara serrata* requires a sheltered spot**

GARDENING WITH **SHRUBS**

PLANT DIRECTORY

4. BERBERIS

Common name Barberry
Family Berberidaceae

This is a huge genus of evergreen and deciduous shrubs. Among those widely available include dwarf varieties suitable for the rock garden, whereas the largest will grow to around 2m (6ft) in height. Berberis have varying shades of fragrant yellow or orange flowers. Most of the deciduous species produce a brilliant show of autumn colour. Berberis have sharp thorns, and some of the larger species can be used as hedging – an attractive deterrent to unwanted visitors.

Popular species and varieties

The *Berberis* is no stranger to our gardens. Several species were introduced early in the 19th century, among them B. *darwinii* (AGM) from China. This is an evergreen with dark green foliage. Its very colourful display of brilliant orange flowers is produced in spring, and is followed by blue-black berries in the autumn. It has a bushy habit, and a mature specimen can reach around 3m (10ft) in height. One of the best species, it can also be used as a hedge.

Another with evergreen foliage is B. x *stenophylla* (AGM), a vigorous shrub producing masses of bright orange-yellow flowers in late spring.

Among the deciduous species is B. *thunbergii* (AGM), a native of Japan that grows to 2m (6ft) in height. The pale yellow flowers appear over the tight green foliage in early summer and are followed by scarlet berries. This is a good species for autumn colour when the foliage turns to bright red. B. t. *atropurpurea* is very similar; its leaves are a dark coppery-purple, and it takes on rich colouring in the autumn.

One of the best of the dwarf berberis is 'Coralina Compacta' (AGM). This very attractive shrub grows to just 30cm (12in) and covers itself with masses of flame-coloured buds that open to yellow flowers in the spring. Finally, one berberis recommended for having a rich autumn colour is B. x *media* 'Red Jewel' (AGM).

Cultivation

Soil type Most well-drained, humus-rich soils are suitable.
Planting This can be done in the autumn or spring. Choose an open sunny spot for the deciduous species and varieties. The evergreen berberis will grow here as well, but will also tolerate lightly shaded areas.
Maintenance General pruning is not necessary. If needed, evergreen varieties should be cut back after flowering. Deciduous berberis should be pruned, if required, in mid-winter.
Propagation The easiest method is to take 7–10cm (3–4in) long cuttings with a heel, in late summer. Place them in an equal peat/coarse sand mixture and overwinter them in a garden frame. In spring move them to a nursery bed, or pot them on individually. In about two years the young plants will be ready to place in their permanent positions.
Pests and diseases Generally trouble free, although berberis can fall victim to honey fungus.

LEFT The foliage of *Berberis* x *media* 'Red Jewel' takes on rich autumn colours

ABOVE **The butterfly bush (*Buddleja davidii*) is a summer spectacle, and easy to grow**

5. BUDDLEJA

Common name Butterfly bush
Family Buddlejaceae

This is one of the best known of all shrubs, noted for its rapid growth, free-flowering habit and attraction for butterflies. It can sometimes be found listed under its old name of *Buddleia*. There are around 100 species, and it is the many named varieties of *Buddleja davidii* that are most often seen in our gardens.

Popular species and varieties

Buddleja davidii is deciduous and a native of China. It grows to 3m (10ft) in height and has a widely spreading habit. It is also very hardy. The masses of tiny honey-scented lilac-purple flowers are produced from mid-summer onwards, and are carried on spikes up to 45cm (18in) long. Among the numerous varieties are 'Black Night' (AGM) with dark purple flowers; 'Empire Blue' (AGM), the nearest to true blue; 'Royal Red' (AGM), a purple-red, and the pure white 'White Profusion' (AGM). Another buddleja that is worth considering is the semi-evergreen *B. globosa* (AGM), commonly known as the 'orange ball tree'. Its globular flower heads 3cm (7in) across are produced in mid to late spring. The shrub, a native of Chile and Peru, was first introduced in 1774.

Cultivation

Soil type Any well-drained soil in an open sunny position.
Planting This can be done in the autumn or spring.
Maintenance It is important to cut back the previous year's growth on *B. davidii*, and its varieties, to within 7–10cm (3–4in) of old wood, in late winter. This will result in strong, erect growth and larger flower spikes. *B. globosa* flowers on the previous season's growth so should be only lightly cut back immediately after flowering.
Propagation These shrubs can be increased by semi-ripe and hardwood cuttings. The former should be taken in summer and the hardwood cuttings in early autumn.
Pests and diseases These shrubs are generally trouble free.

ABOVE **Dwarf box is ideal for edging as it will withstand frequent trimming**

6. BUXUS

Common name Box
Family Buxaceae

These shrubs are grown principally for their foliage. They are widely used for edging and topiary, or simply as clipped specimens. The plants have the ability to withstand regular trimming. There are numerous species of common box (*Buxus sempervirens*), and there are some excellent named varieties with variegated foliage.

Popular species and varieties

Buxus sempervirens (AGM) forms a neat bushy shrub with glossy dark green foliage; the fragrant pale green flowers are inconspicuous, appearing in early spring. 'Suffruticosa' (AGM) is compact and slow growing – ideal for edging. A popular variety of this box is 'Aureovariegata', the green leaves of which are striped and mottled creamy yellow. 'Elegantissima' (AGM) is another splendid choice, the green leaves having irregular, creamy white margins.

Cultivation

Soil type Most well-drained fertile soils are suitable.
Planting Box will grow well in lightly shaded areas; if in full sun or dry poor soil, this may lead to poor foliage colour and scorching.
Maintenance Regular trimming where necessary. In the case of young plants used for edging, stopping the leading shoots will encourage bushy growth.
Propagation Take semi-ripe cuttings in the summer, rooting them in a garden frame.
Pests and diseases Fungus diseases can attack box. Treat with fungicide when identified. Occasionally, scale insects can become established. Deal with these by using a suitable insecticide.

GARDENING WITH **SHRUBS**

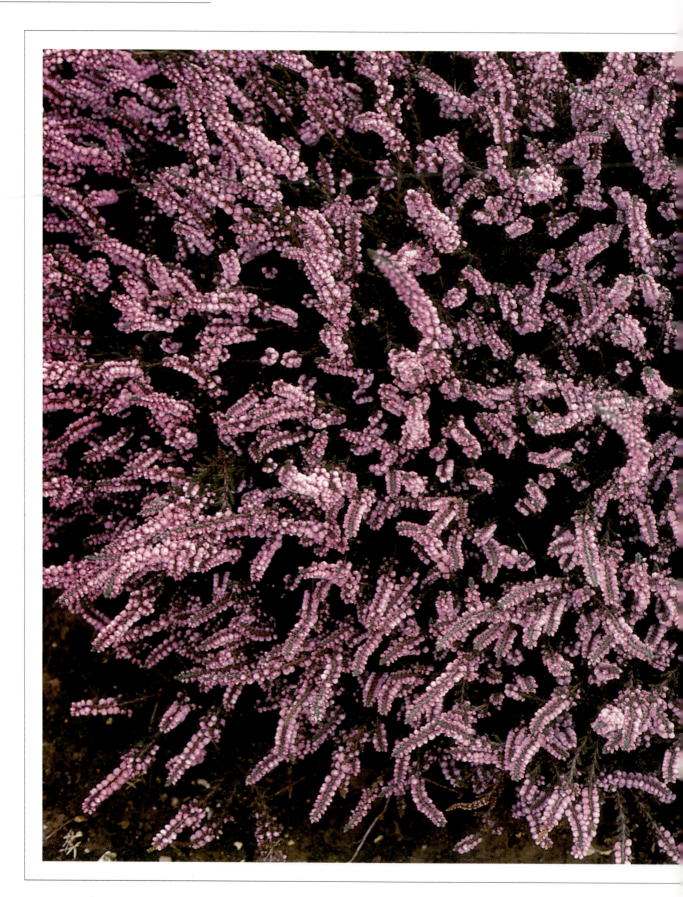

PLANT DIRECTORY

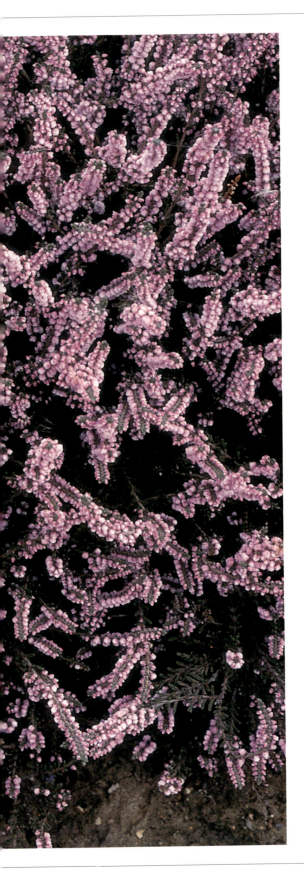

7. CALLUNA

Common name Heather, Ling
Family Ericaceae

All plants in the *Calluna* genus need acid soil conditions, and they are excellent for use as ground cover. They vary considerably in height – depending on variety – the tallest reaching 60cm (24in). Flowering takes place in the summer or autumn.

Popular species and varieties

There is just one species, *Calluna vulgaris*, and hundreds of named varieties, with many types of coloured foliage including gold, grey, bronze, red and purple. Some of those with green foliage change colour during autumn. Flowers are single or double in varying shades of white, pink or purple.

Among the most popular is 'H. E. Beale' which covers itself with masses of double bright pink flowers in late summer and early autumn, and grows to around 45cm (18in) in height. 'Ruth Sparkes' is a compact plant with yellow foliage and double white flowers. Another that always attracts attention is 'Beoley Gold', the foliage in this case a rich gold, setting off the white flowers. One variety that will usually carry on the display later in the autumn is 'Kinlochruel' (AGM); it does not exceed 30cm (12in) in height and has lovely double pink flowers. With so many from which to choose it is always a good idea to make your choice when the plants are in bloom.

Cultivation

Soil type This must be well drained and of an acid type. Adding peat to the soil at planting time is beneficial.
Planting Best carried out in the autumn or spring. Plant so the foliage rests on the ground. Spacing will depend on the variety. Ensure new plants do not suffer from drought during their first year.
Maintenance There is little work required throughout the season. Trim over in late winter to remove dead flowers and encourage new growth. Cut back any long straggly stems to keep the plant tidy.
Propagation The easiest method of propagation is by taking cuttings with a heel in early to mid-summer. Pinch out the tip and place in a garden frame. Callunas can also be propagated by layering.
Pests and diseases Callunas can be attacked by a fungus disease that causes die-back. Should this happen it is best to lift the plant and destroy it.

LEFT *Calluna* 'H. E. Beale' flowers in the autumn and requires an acid soil

GARDENING WITH **SHRUBS**

8. CAMELLIA

Common name none
Family Theaceae

The *Camellia* is unquestionably one of the most popular of all evergreen shrubs. Flowering early in the year, its blooms can be damaged by cold winds, and after frost if in a position where early morning sun causes quick thawing. There are a considerable number of species, but those usually seen in our gardens are from legions of named varieties.

The foliage of camellias is oval, glossy and attractive when not in flower. The blooms range from single to semi or fully double, and come is a variety of attractive shades of pink, red and white.

Popular species and varieties

The majority of camellias available are varieties of *C. japonica*, which originates from Japan and Korea. It forms a sizeable shrub 2–3m (6–9ft) in height, and flowers from mid-winter through until mid-spring. Among these are 'Adolphe Audusson' (AGM) with its semi-double, 10–12cm (4–5in) wide, red blooms. One noted for its peony-like flowers is the scarlet-red 'Miss Charleston' (AGM).

Another group of popular varieties is listed as *C. x williamsii*. These include the large silvery pink 'Donation' (AGM) and soft pink 'J. C. Williams' (AGM). 'Taylor's Perfection' is another good choice, with pink blooms.

Cultivation

Soil type Camellias are not difficult to grow, if you have a well-drained, lime-free soil. When planting, incorporate some peat.
Planting Positioning is important, as camellias require a cool root run. Wherever possible, select a westerly or northerly aspect, ideally against a wall or backed by trees and shrubs. Provide shelter from cold icy winds. After a night-time frost, an early sun can easily damage blooms. Should this happen, however, there are usually unopened buds that will give flowers later. Camellias can be grown in alkaline areas in containers of ericaceous compost. Choose from among the more compact varieties, and water only with collected rainwater.
Maintenance Newly planted camellias should be staked until they are well established.
Pruning This is not generally necessary. Any straggly shoots can be cut back during mid-spring, as long as it doesn't harm the flowering potential. This is also a good time to give a mulch of well-rotted manure, leafmould or garden compost.
Pests and diseases Birds will sometimes damage early flowers. Another problem sometimes experienced is 'bud drop'. This is normally caused by frost damage, or by the soil being too dry. Scale insects can be a problem; treat with a suitable insecticide.

LEFT *Camellia* 'J.C. Williams' – a single pink variety

GARDENING WITH **SHRUBS**

PLANT DIRECTORY

9. CEANOTHUS

Common name Californian lilac
Family Rhamnaceae

These attractive shrubs are native to North America, in particular the state of California, hence its common name. It is, however, very different to the popular common lilac (forms of *Syringa*). There are 50 species with both evergreen and deciduous forms among them. All ceanothus are sun lovers. The evergreen varieties should be grown with the protection of a sheltered warm wall – they are not successful in open parts of the garden where they are subjected to cold winds. The deciduous forms are generally hardier and can be planted in a border, but even here the plants may be damaged in very cold areas.

Most ceanothus flower from mid to late spring, the blooms being varying shades of blue. Pink varieties are to be found among the later-flowering deciduous forms.

Popular species and varieties

If space is not a problem then the deep blue *C. arboreus* is worth considering; it can produce a sizeable shrub. 'Trewithin Blue' is even better, noted for its richer colouring. It blooms in mid to late spring, and often produces a second flush in late summer.

Most of the ceanothus seen in our gardens are named forms. Three to look out for are 'Blue Cushion', a very deep blue with a neat spreading habit; 'Blue Mound', well known for its dense clusters of bright blue flowers in mid to late spring, and the deep blue 'Cynthia Postan', known for its free-flowering habit and good bushy form.

The majority grow into sizeable shrubs. There are some with a low-growing habit, including the vigorous *C. thyrsiflorus* var. *repens* (AGM) which reaches around 60–90cm (24–36in) in height. In late spring and early summer it is covered with terminal clusters of light blue flowers. It's an ideal plant for growing on a bank or over a low wall.

Among the deciduous ceanothus is 'Gloire de Versailles' (AGM). In mid-summer this produces large panicles of pale blue flowers – a very good subject for the border.

Cultivation

Soil type Light humus-rich soils in a sunny spot are ideal for these shrubs. Some can show signs of chlorosis in soils that are alkaline.
Planting This can be carried out during autumn or spring (the latter is preferable, as they will establish quicker as temperatures rise).
Maintenance The evergreens require little pruning. The spring-flowering plants can be trimmed immediately after flowering, if necessary. Those that flower later should be trimmed in mid-spring, if required. The deciduous forms should be cut back hard in early spring to within 7cm (3in) of the old wood.
Propagation Take cuttings with a heel during mid-summer. Insert them in a pot containing an equal quantity of peat and coarse sand. Overwinter them in a garden frame. Pot them on individually into 12cm (5in) pots the following spring. The young plants should be ready for their permanent positions in autumn.
Pests and diseases Generally there are few problems. Scale insects, if found, can be treated with insecticide. Die-back of shoots is usually caused by frost damage.

LEFT There are numerous forms of *Ceanothus*, in varying shades of blue

ABOVE *Ceratostigma plumbaginoides* is useful for its late flowering

10. CERATOSTIGMA

Common name Hardy plumbago
Family Plumbaginaceae

The *Ceratostigma* genus comprises deciduous dwarf shrubs that flower from mid-summer to early autumn. The bright blue flowers nestle among the sharply pointed deep green summer leaves, which take on tints of red and copper in autumn.

Popular species and varieties

There are three species widely available. First there is *C. griffithii*, a native of the Eastern Himalayas, with small blue flowers. The most widely known is *C. willmottianum* (AGM), which originates from China and flowers in late summer. It can often be cut to the ground during the winter by sharp frosts, but new growth usually appears in the spring.

C. plumbaginoides (AGM) also comes from China. This is a neat plant that can be grown on the rock garden, used as ground cover, or allowed to trail over a wall. It produces terminal clusters of blue flowers from mid-summer until the first frosts. The foliage takes on autumnal tints.

Cultivation

Soil type Most humus-rich, well-drained soils are suitable.
Planting Choose an open, sunny spot, but one that is not subjected to cold winds.
Maintenance No regular pruning is necessary. In late winter any old straggly shoots should be cut back to ground level.
Propagation Take cuttings with a heel from sun-ripened shoots, during mid-summer.
Pests and diseases Generally trouble free.

ABOVE *Chaenomeles* 'Crimson & Gold': early flowering, and ideal when grown against a wall

11. CHAENOMELES

Common name Japonica
Family Rosaceae

The various forms of *Chaenomeles* are noted for their early flowering. Easily grown in most soils, it is the many named varieties of *C. speciosa* that are the most familiar in our gardens. The species itself was introduced from its native Japan in the mid 19th century.

Popular species and varieties

There are numerous varieties of these colourful shrubs. One of the best known is 'Crimson & Gold' (AGM); its red flowers are highlighted by the golden anthers. 'Moerloosei' (AGM) is another old favourite, with pale pink and white blooms. Others to look out for are 'Pink Lady' (AGM), a lovely clear rose pink, and 'Elly Mossel' with orange-red flowers. The deep scarlet 'Nicoline' (AGM) makes a fine show early in the year.

Cultivation

Soil type These easy going shrubs will grow in most fertile soils.
Planting This can be carried out in the autumn or spring. Choose a sheltered spot, ideally against a wall. Chaenomeles are happy in full sun or lightly shaded areas.
Maintenance When grown against a wall, when flowering has finished in mid-spring, cut back the previous year's growth to two or three buds. When grown as a bush, little pruning is required, with the exception of cutting out any crowded branches, again after flowering.
Propagation The best method is by taking semi-ripe cuttings with a heel in mid-summer. Layering of suitable shoots can be done during the summer months.
Pests and diseases The flowers can be attacked by birds. In very alkaline soils chlorosis can cause yellowing of the foliage.

ABOVE *Choisya ternata* 'Sundance' has rich-coloured foliage, best grown in a sheltered spot

12. CHOISYA

Common name Mexican orange blossom
Family Rutaceae

During mid-spring these aromatic evergreen shrubs clothe themselves with masses of starry white flowers. They are noted for their strong orange-like fragrance, hence their common name. In most dry seasons these are followed by a second, albeit smaller, flush of blooms in autumn.

They are happy in full sun or a lightly shaded area, in most fertile soil conditions, and are ideally suited to town gardens.

Popular species and varieties

As the common name indicates, *Choisya ternata* (AGM) is a native of Mexico. It was first introduced to European gardens in 1825. The dark, shiny leaves are three-parted, a perfect foil for the cluster of pure white flowers. Ideally it should be grown in a position where it is not subjected to cold winds, as the foliage can be damaged in the winter. One impressive form that made its debut in 1986 is 'Sundance' (AGM), with bright yellow foliage. This should be grown in a sunny spot, and is a more compact shrub than the species.

One noted for its free-flowering habit is 'Aztec Pearl' (AGM). It has elongated leaves of rich green, and the backs of the white petals are flushed with pink.

Cultivation

Soil type These shrubs are happy in most humus-rich soils.
Planting This is best done in the spring when they will become established quickly as soil temperatures rise. Autumn planting leads to the possibility of damage to the young foliage during the winter. In cold districts it is wise to plant them where they will receive shelter from a south-facing wall.
Maintenance No pruning is required. Any straggly shoots can be removed after flowering. Any growth damage by frost should be cut out during late winter. New shoots will soon appear.
Propagation Root semi-ripe cuttings in an equal peat/sand mix, and place them in a garden frame.
Pests and diseases They are generally trouble free.

ABOVE *Cistus* x *purpureus* produces a long succession of flowers

13. CISTUS

Common name Rock rose/Sun rose
Family Cistaceae

Cistus are free-flowering shrubs with short-lived blooms, lasting for just one day.

However, such is the profusion of buds, plants look little different the following morning!

They come from southern Europe, particularly the Mediterranean region, so they require a warm sunny spot in well-drained soil. They are not successful in shade or where soil conditions are heavy.

Popular species and varieties

C. albidus has been grown in our gardens for over 300 years; it is short-lived, and is not reliably hardy in severe winters. The lovely light pink flowers are a redeeming feature however, blooming from late spring to mid-summer. *C.* x *cyprius* is one of the hardiest species and grows to 160cm (60in) with a rather lax growth habit. The large white flowers have a distinctive maroon-crimson blotch in the centre. Another old stager is *C. laurifolius* (AGM), noted for its upright habit and profusion of pure white blooms. One of the most spectacular is *C.* x *purpureus* (AGM). It has been around for a great many years. The masses of large, rich pink flowers with maroon blotches, on neat 120cm (48in) high bushes, are most eyecatching.

Cultivation

Soil type Full sun and well-drained, even fairly poor soils, are all that is required.
Planting This is best done in spring. Choose sturdy young plants, as older specimens are more difficult to establish. Select a spot where they are not subjected to cold winds.
Maintenance Pruning is not required. Any unwanted shoots can be cut back lightly in spring. These plants do not respond well to being cut back hard, so there is a danger of some loss if you do this.
Propagation Root semi-ripe cuttings in summer.
Pests and diseases Generally trouble free. Frost can cause damage, resulting in die-back. Cut out any affected shoots in the spring.

GARDENING WITH SHRUBS

14. CLEMATIS

Common name Virgin's bower
Family Ranunculaceae

Forms of *Clematis* are, unquestionably, the most popular of all climbing shrubs. There are two basic types: the spring-flowering species with smaller blooms, and the ever-popular large-flowered hybrids that bloom from late spring to early autumn, depending on variety.

Popular species and varieties

One species that makes a fine show in the spring is *Clematis montana*, producing masses of white flowers. Originating from the Himalayas, it is a vigorous plant that can grow to 5m (15ft) in height and spread. There are several named forms of *C. montana*, among them 'Elizabeth' (AGM), a soft pink. Another clematis that blooms in spring is the European *C. alpina* (AGM). The flowers are pendulous, cup-shaped and violet-blue. There are a number of varieties and one of the best is 'Blue Dancer', a pale blue with long, narrow, twisted petals.

Early summer is when *C. macropetala* starts to flower, with nodding blue bell-shaped blooms. This species originates from China and Siberia, and grows to around 4m (12ft) in height. 'Maidwell Hall' (AGM) is a good form, with deep blue flowers. 'Markham's Pink' (AGM) is a rich rose pink.

One species useful for later flowering is *C. tangutica*, producing yellow bell-shaped blooms in mid-summer.

For many, it is the large-flowered hybrids that have the most charm. These generally grow to around 3m (10ft) in height, with flowers, depending on variety, 10–15cm (4–6in) across. One is certainly spoilt for choice, with hundreds of varieties from which to choose. 'Nelly Moser' (AGM) is perhaps the best known, its large blooms being pink tinged with white, with a distinctive red stripe on each petal. Another with a free-flowering habit is 'Mrs Cholmondley' (AGM), a lovely pale blue. One that never fails to attract attention, with its large pure white blooms, is 'Marie Boisselot' (AGM). There are many nurserymen specializing in these plants; their descriptive, well-illustrated catalogues give an indication of the range available.

LEFT *Clematis montana* **'Elizabeth' – a rich pink form of this well-known climber**

Cultivation

Soil type Clematis require good, well-drained, humus-rich soil.

Planting This can be done in the autumn or spring. Positioning is important, as clematis need an open spot, but with the base of the stem and the roots shaded from strong sun. This shade can be provided either by a low-growing shrub, or simply some large stones placed strategically. The junction where the stem merges with the root should be around 2.5cm (1in) below soil level.

Maintenance Pruning – when and how this is done depends on type. In the case of the spring-flowering varieties, prune immediately after flowering, generally carried out when space is restricted. Take out all the flowered shoots, and tie in the new growth. Those in this group include *C. alpina*, *C. macropetala* and *C. montana*.

The large-flowered hybrids that bloom in early summer should be pruned from mid to late winter. Shorten to the first pair of strong buds.

The varieties that flower from early summer should have their growth cut back hard in late winter, to a pair of strong buds 1m (3ft) or less above ground level.

With all clematis you should water freely in dry weather, and mulch with well-rotted compost in the spring.

Propagation Take semi-ripe cuttings 10cm (4in) long, in mid-summer. Space these cuttings around the edge of a pot containing an equal mixture of peat and sharp sand. Place them in a frame, preferably a propagating frame, with bottom heat. When rooted, pot them individually and overwinter them in a frost-free greenhouse. Move them into larger pots in the spring. The new plants should be ready to go out in the autumn.

Pests and diseases Aphids, earwigs and slugs can attack new growth; control with appropriate preparations. Clematis wilt: This fungal disease shows itself by the sudden collapse of the plant. If this happens, cut it out immediately. Usually, new shoots will emerge later in the season or the following spring.

Mildew: This can be present; treat with a fungicide. Virus-infected clematis will show mottled and distorted foliage. Unfortunately there is no cure, so the plant should be dug out and burnt.

ABOVE *Convolvulus cneorum* is not grown as often as it deserves

15. CONVOLVULUS

Common name Shrubby bindweed
Family Convolvulaceae

The common name for *Convolvulus cneorum* (AGM) should in no way discourage anyone from growing this free-flowering, low-growing shrub. A plant from the warm parts of Europe, it should be grown in a sheltered, sunny spot, ideally where it receives protection from the elements by a south-facing wall.

Popular species and varieties

Convolvulus cneorum (AGM) grows to around 45cm (18in) in height and seldom spreads to much more than 60cm (24in). The foliage has a silvery appearance, the large white flowers, striped with pink on the reverse, appear in mid-spring and are 5cm (2in) across. It will usually bloom at frequent intervals until late summer. This convolvulus is an ideal subject for the front of a flower border, and is most suited to a sheltered spot on a large rock garden.

Cultivation

Soil type Well-drained, light, sandy soil is ideal.
Planting This is best done in the spring; choose a sunny, sheltered spot.
Maintenance There is little work required, as pruning is not essential, with the exception of cutting out any weak or straggly growth in the spring.
Propagation Take semi-ripe cuttings with a heel in early to mid-summer. Root them in the usual way, and overwinter them in a frost-free greenhouse. It is a good idea to keep a few young plants coming on, to replace any winter casualties.
Pests and diseases Generally trouble free.

16. CORDYLINE

Common name Cabbage tree
Family Agavaceae

These striking plants, with their narrow sword-like foliage, have become very popular in recent years. They are best grown as specimen plants on a patio where they can be moved undercover for the winter. In mild districts they can be grown outdoors in a sunny sheltered spot, where they are not subjected to cold winds.

Popular species and varieties

Those most commonly seen are varieties of *Cordyline australis* (AGM), a native of New Zealand and Australia. Those with coloured foliage include 'Torbay Dazzler' with broad cream stripes and margins, and 'Purple Tower' with broader leaves of a rich, plum purple. Others to look for are 'Albertii' (AGM), with foliage striped red, pink and cream, and 'Torbay Red' with dark red leaves. The forms with coloured leaves are slightly less hardy than the straight species (which has mid-green foliage).

Cultivation

Soil type If grown outdoors, a well-drained, light soil is required; these plants will not tolerate cold, wet conditions. If growing in containers, use a loam-based compost and provide plenty of drainage. From late spring to early autumn a fortnightly feed of a balanced general fertilizer is beneficial. Ensure that the plants are not subjected to drought, especially in hot weather. Move them into a frost-free greenhouse for the winter months.
Planting If you have a suitable spot, cordylines are best planted in the spring. Remember they are sun lovers and require a spot sheltered from strong cold winds.
Maintenance There is little required except to water freely in dry weather. No pruning is necessary. Remove any dead lower leaves.
Propagation Any well-rooted suckers can be removed in the spring, potted up and grown on. Alternatively, sow seed in John Innes seed compost during early spring, in gentle heat. Prick out the seedlings to individual pots, and grow them on in the usual way.
Pests and diseases Generally trouble free.

ABOVE *Cordyline australis* 'Torbay Red' – architectural plants that have become very popular

GARDENING WITH **SHRUBS**

PLANT DIRECTORY

17. CORNUS

Common name Dogwood
Family Cornaceae

Within this family are numerous shrubs, trees and ground-covering sub-shrubs. They generally fall into two groups: those grown for their attractive coloured stems, and the flowering 'dogwoods'.

Popular species and varieties

Of those grown for their invaluable winter colour, one that is most widely grown is *Cornus alba*, a vigorous, suckering, upright-growing shrub. 'Sibirica' (AGM) has stunning coral-red stems in winter; it is also sometimes listed as 'Westonbirt'. Another to consider with the same stem colouring, but with variegated foliage, is 'Sibirica Variegata' (AGM). 'Spaethii' (AGM) has golden variegated leaves and red stems that are most eye-catching in winter. One form that is very popular is 'Aurea', with golden leaves. These cornus also take on attractive autumn leaf tints. Another cornus noted for its winter stem colour is the bright yellow-green *C. stolonifera* 'Flaviramea' (AGM).

One member of the family that is a splendid addition to the winter garden, this time not for its stem colour but for the umbels of small yellow flowers produced in profusion in late winter, is *Cornus mas*. It is perhaps better known to many gardeners by its common name of Cornelian cherry. This is a vigorous spreading deciduous shrub. Its flowers are produced on bare stems. The blooms are followed in late summer by fleshy, bright red fruits.

A cornus that stands out well either as a specimen or in a border is *C. controversa* 'Variegata' (AGM); its foliage is attractively marked with white. The flowering dogwood (*Cornus florida*) is a deciduous shrub or small tree. There are a number of excellent varieties:

'Cherokee Chief' (AGM) with rich ruby-pink bracts; 'Cloud Nine', the bracts in this case white, and 'Rainbow', also with white bracts – its name refers to the dark green leaves with yellow-green margins that turn to purple-red in the autumn. *Cornus florida* is noted for its rich autumn colour.

One hybrid that grows into a sizeable shrub is 'Eddie's White Wonder' (AGM). It is deciduous and of upright habit. The rounded white bracts are produced in mid-spring, wreathing the branches. In autumn it has a further surprise in store; the foliage turns to bright orange.

A member of the cornus family grown as a ground-covering plant is the creeping dogwood (*C. canadensis*) (AGM). This sub-shrub was introduced into Europe from North America in 1774. The low-growing foliage is almost hidden by white flowers.

Cultivation

Soil type Most cornus are happy in humus-rich, well-drained soil. The exceptions are *C. florida* and *C. canadensis* – both dislike alkaline conditions.
Planting This is best done in late winter or early spring. Choose a sunny spot, although most will be successful in a lightly shaded area.
Maintenance Cornus grown for their colourful stems should be cut back in the spring to within a few inches of ground level. This should first be done in their second year and annually thereafter, and will result in a much neater plant and rich colouring on new growth. Other members of the family do not generally require pruning.
Propagation Semi-ripe cuttings with a heel may be taken in early to mid-summer. Root in the normal way.
Pests and diseases Normally trouble free.

LEFT The rich yellow foliage of *Cornus alba* 'Aurea' provides a good contrast to many other shrubs

GARDENING WITH **SHRUBS**

ABOVE *Corylopsis sinensis* – free-flowering, but must have acid soil

18. CORYLOPSIS

Common name Winter hazel
Family Hamamelidaceae

There are seven species of these attractive early flowering shrubs. While they are easily grown, they do require neutral or acid soil conditions, and some shelter from cold winds.

Popular species and varieties

Corylopsis sinensis var. *sinensis* (AGM) is a medium-sized shrub formerly listed as *C. willmottiae*, a native of Western China and introduced to Europe in 1900. In early spring, before the leaves appear, it produces showy racemes of yellow flowers. One species that grows to around 2m (6ft) in height is *C. pauciflora* (AGM), which forms a densely branched shrub. The primrose-yellow flowers are fragrant and carried in short tassels.

Cultivation

Soil type Lime-free and well drained.
Planting This can be done in the autumn or spring. Avoid 'frost pockets' and find a sheltered spot where the plants are not subjected to icy winds. Flowering early in the year, they can easily be damaged by frost. They can be grown in sun or light shade.
Maintenance There is little work required. Pruning is not necessary, only remove unwanted or damaged branches after flowering.
Propagation Take cuttings 7–10cm (3–4in) in length, with a heel, in early to mid-summer. Treat in the usual manner. Alternatively, layer shoots.
Pests and diseases It is unlikely that any problems will be experienced.

ABOVE *Cotinus coggyria* is known as the smoke tree, and has been in cultivation since 1656

19. COTINUS

Common name Smoke bush
Family Anacardiaceae

The deciduous shrub *Cotinus coggyria* (AGM) has gained its common name due to its plume-like inflorescences which, by autumn, have turned a smoke-grey.

Popular species and varieties

Cotinus coggyria (AGM) has been an old favourite since its introduction to Europe in 1656. It has rounded mid-green leaves that take on fine autumn colour. There are a considerable number of forms: 'Royal Purple' (AGM) has deep wine-red foliage which, as autumn approaches, takes on a more reddish hue. Also similar is 'Notcutt's Variety'. The popular 'Velvet Cloak' has deep red-purple foliage that colours well in autumn. One must not overlook the hybrid 'Flame' (AGM), which produces clusters of pink flowers. Its main attraction is in the autumn when the leaves turn a brilliant orange-red before they fall.

Cultivation

Soil type Most well-drained soils are suitable. In rich conditions these shrubs will take on reduced autumn tints.
Planting This can be carried out during autumn or spring. Choose an open, sunny spot.
Maintenance No general pruning is required. Any long, straggly growth can be shortened or removed in early spring.
Pests and diseases Mildew can become a problem; spray with a suitable fungicide.

GARDENING WITH **SHRUBS**

PLANT DIRECTORY

20. COTONEASTER

Common name none
Family Rosaceae

There are a considerable number of these popular ornamental shrubs, both evergreen and deciduous. They range from mat-forming types that are ideal for ground cover, to sizeable shrubs and trees.

Popular species and varieties

One very popular low-growing cotoneaster is *C. conspicuus* 'Decorus' (AGM), which is a good subject for covering banks or difficult spots. In early summer it produces masses of small, white flowers along the entire length of its branches. These are followed by equally as many long-lasting bright red berries. Also very useful for the same purpose is *C. horizontalis* (AGM). Here again with white flowers, but the orange-red berries are accompanied by richly coloured autumn foliage.

Much larger, in due course growing into a small tree, is *C. frigidus* 'Cornubia' (AGM). This has dark foliage and masses of red berries. 'Hybridus Pendulus' is another that is widely available. It has glossy foliage and white flowers on long, prostrate branches; in autumn and winter it carries masses of red berries. It can be grown on a stem to form a small weeping tree. The majority of cotoneasters produce red berries, but there are exceptions, one being *C. salicifolius* 'Rothschildianus' (AGM) with yellow fruits.

Cultivation

Soil type Most well-drained garden soils, but they will not tolerate wet conditions.
Planting Plant in autumn or spring, in an open, sunny spot.
Maintenance Regular pruning is not required. Unwanted or damaged branches can be removed: with deciduous varieties this should be carried out in mid-winter, the evergreens should be tackled in early spring.
Propagation Cuttings of 7cm (3in) in length, with a heel, should be taken in mid-summer. Root them in the usual manner.
Pests and diseases Aphid and scale insect attacks can be dealt with by insecticide. Cotoneasters can also be subject to certain fungal diseases which in mild cases cause die-back, and in severe cases cause the plant to fail completely.

LEFT *Cotoneaster conspicuus* – grown for its colourful berries

GARDENING WITH SHRUBS

21.
CRINODENDRON

Common name
Chilean lantern tree
Family Elaeocarpaceae

Attractive as *Crinodendron hookerianum* (AGM) is, not everyone has the opportunity to grow it. Requiring a warm, sheltered spot where it is not subjected to strong winds, it really only succeeds in mild districts and on lime-free soil.

Popular species and varieties

Crinodendron hookerianum (AGM) was introduced to Europe in 1848 from Chile. It grows to a height of 3m (10ft), with an upright, dense, bushy habit. The evergreen leaves are dark green, leathery and toothed. The flower buds start to form in the autumn. The main feature – attractive coral-red lantern-shaped flowers – is carried on 7cm (3in) long pendent stalks from mid to late spring.

Cultivation

Soil type Lime-free, moist and well-drained.
Planting Plant in early to mid-spring in a lightly shaded spot, ideally where it is sheltered by a south-facing wall.
Maintenance Any unwanted branches can be removed in the spring, otherwise pruning is not necessary.
Propagation Increase by taking cuttings with a heel, using half-ripe shoots, in early to mid-summer. Root and pot on, always using a lime-free compost. Young plants should be ready for planting out in their second year.
Pests and diseases Pest attacks are unlikely, but this shrub can fall victim to honey fungus disease.

LEFT The lantern tree (*Crinodendron hookerianum*) is so named because of its lantern-shaped flowers

PLANT DIRECTORY

ABOVE **In the spring,** Cytisus **'Compact Crimson' covers itself with flowers**

22. CYTISUS

Common name Broom
Family Papilionaceae

Few people could fail to notice a *Cytisus* **in full flower, covered with masses of pea-like blooms. Choose from prostrate shrubs to bushes of 4m (12ft) or more in height.**

Popular species and varieties

Most cytisus seen in our gardens are varieties or hybrids. Among the yellows are 'Porlock' (AGM), a splendid choice. This forms a sizeable semi-evergreen bush which covers its branches with masses of highly fragrant golden-yellow blooms. It requires a sheltered spot. 'Burwoodii' (AGM) is another to look out for, this time with late spring to early summer flowers of cerise, the wings of which are deep crimson, edged with yellow. One that can be relied upon to make a fine show is 'Compact Crimson'. Very different in habit is the pineapple broom (*Cytisus battandieri*) (AGM). This is a good, deciduous wall shrub, growing to 4m (12ft) or more. The pineapple-scented blooms of golden yellow are produced in cone-shaped clusters in late spring to early summer.

Cultivation

Soil type Well-drained soil, preferably of poor, sandy type.
Planting Cytisus resent root disturbance, and are often short-lived. Plant them in a sunny corner, the best time being autumn or spring.
Maintenance Regular pruning is not required for most types. Those that flower on previous years' growth can be cut back to half after flowering. Do not cut into old, brown wood.
Pests and diseases None likely.

23. DAPHNE

Common name None
Family Thymelaceae

One of the best known members of this family is *Daphne mezereum* which covers itself with fragrant purple-red flowers on bare stems from mid to late winter, a time when any form of colour is very welcome in the garden.

The genus contains approximately 50 species, both evergreen and deciduous. Within their ranks are low-growing, dwarf and small shrubs. Daphnes are particularly noted for their sweet scent.

Popular species and varieties

Daphne mezereum is to be found naturally in Europe, Turkey and other parts of the Middle East. It forms a neat bush which, in mature specimens, can reach 1.8m (5ft). The flowers are followed by scarlet berries – as with all members of the family, these are poisonous.

There is also a white form, *D. mezereum alba* – the berries in this case are yellow. Also flowering early is *D. odora* 'Aureomarginata', a native of China and Japan. It also grows to around 1.8m (5ft) but has a lax habit. The pale green leaves have narrow creamy margins.

One daphne that does not commence flowering until mid-spring is *D. tangutica* 'Retusa Group', formerly listed as *D. retusa*. This produces purplish-red blooms on bushes of lax habit. Vivid bright red berries follow.

There are a number of daphnes that are ideal subjects for the rock garden, and among these is the garland flower (*D. cneorum*). This evergreen shrub has a prostrate habit, growing to 15cm (6in) in height with richly scented rose-pink flowers in mid to late spring. One named form is 'Eximia' (AGM) – widely regarded as being superior, this grows slightly larger and has very colourful blooms which almost completely hide the plant.

Cultivation

Soil type Most well-drained, humus-rich soils are suitable, including those of an alkaline type.
Planting In autumn or spring. Daphnes are happy in sun or lightly shaded areas.
Maintenance Pruning is not required. Any damaged growth can be removed in late winter.
Propagation Cuttings of around 7cm (3in) in length, with a heel, should be taken in early to mid-summer. Choose non-flowering, semi-ripe shoots. Treat in the usual manner. The young plants should be ready to plant out after their second winter.
Pests and diseases Aphids can attack young growth; treat as soon as seen with an insecticide.

ABOVE *Daphne mezereum* – a shrub that produces early flowering on bare stems

ABOVE *Deutzia x kalmiiflora* is a useful shrub for the smaller garden

24. DEUTZIA

Common name None
Family Hydrangeaceae

These medium-sized deciduous shrubs are noted for their free-flowering habit. They are hardy, but late frost can damage new growth.

Popular species and varieties

Deutzia x hybrida is a group that includes some splendid varieties with rich colours. Among these are: 'Mont Rose' (AGM), with a free-flowering habit and graceful heads of warm-pink flowers; 'Magicien', a rich lilac, edged with white, and as a contrast, 'Joconde', with purplish buds and white blooms. These hybrids are old stagers, raised in France many years ago and still widely available.

Early summer is when *D. x elegantissima* 'Rosealind' (AGM) produces arching sprays of lovely rose-pink flowers. *D. scabra* was brought over in the 19th century from the Far East. This has a number of varieties: 'Pride of Rochester' is among the best known, with double white flowers delicately tinged pink. One certainly not to overlook is *D. setchuenensis* var. *corymbiflora* (AGM) with masses of tiny white star-like flowers in summer.

Cultivation

Soil type Most well-drained, humus-rich soils are suitable.
Planting This can be done in the autumn or spring. Choose a spot that is not north-facing, and which is protected from icy winds. Sun or light shade.
Maintenance Cut back old stems immediately after flowering has finished, to encourage new growth.
Pests and diseases Generally trouble-free.

GARDENING WITH **SHRUBS**

86

PLANT DIRECTORY

25. ERICA

Common name Heath, Heather
Family Ericaceae

Heathers have much to offer, and with careful choice it is possible to have plants in bloom throughout the year. Whilst a bed given over to these plants exclusively can be stunning, and it is arguably the best way to display them, this is not to everyone's taste and not everyone can afford to set aside the required amount of space. This should in no way detract from these colourful plants, as they can be used with great effect in the border. Compact varieties are perfect for the rock garden, and many forms are successful simply as ground cover.

One important consideration is the type of soil you have. Some forms of *Erica* require acid conditions. Fortunately this does not apply to them all – the winter-flowering heathers, including *E. carnea*, will grow in alkaline soils.

Popular species and varieties

Among the best known ericas are the numerous varieties of *E. carnea*, which grow to around 23cm (9in) in height and, depending on the variety, can flower from late autumn to early spring. There are a whole host from which to choose, among them old favourites such as 'King George', rose-pink; 'Springwood White' (AGM), and 'Pink Spangles' (AGM) with rosy-red flowers.

Also tolerant of lime, and winter-flowering, is *E. x darleyensis* which grows to 60cm (24in). Among the forms available are 'Arthur Johnson' (AGM), rose pink, and 'Furzey' (AGM), rich pink. Grown for their summer flowers are numerous varieties of the bell heather (*E. cinerea*). These are lime-haters, growing 23–30cm (9–12in) high. Among them are 'C. G. Best' (AGM), rose pink, and the deep beetroot-red 'Velvet Night' (AGM). The Cornish heath (*E. vagans*) grows to 60cm (24in) and will not tolerate lime. 'Cornish Cream' (AGM), with long racemes of white flowers, is a good choice. The tree heather (*E. arborea*) grows to 3m (10ft) or more in ideal conditions; here again it is a lime-hater. One noted for its bright golden foliage and white flowers is 'Albert's Gold' (AGM).

Cultivation

Soil type The preferred soil type varies between the species, but it is safe to say that most require peaty, acid conditions. The exceptions are the ericas that flower in winter or early spring, which will tolerate alkaline soils to which peat has been incorporated.

Planting This can be done in the autumn or spring. The plants appreciate an open, sunny spot. Plant so that the stem is buried, with foliage resting on the soil. Irrespective of type, always incorporate peat at the planting stage, as this will help to improve water-holding capacity on light soils. Heavy conditions can be improved by incorporating sharp sand or grit. Keep plants well watered, especially in dry spells.

Maintenance The plants should be trimmed over as soon as flowering has finished. Remove any straggly shoots, but avoid cutting into old wood. The dead flowers on some of the summer-blooming varieties, with their varying brown shades, are ornamental during the winter and can be left until the spring.

Propagation Cuttings with a heel, taken between early summer and early autumn.

Pests and diseases Normally, no problems are experienced. A fungal disease causing die-back can attack plants.

LEFT *Erica arborea* 'Albert's Gold' is a richly coloured form of tree heath

GARDENING WITH SHRUBS

ABOVE *Euonymus* 'Emerald Gold', an easy-to-grow evergreen, raised in the USA

26. EUONYMUS

Common name Spindleberry
Family Celastraceae

The two most popular members of the genus are variegated evergreen shrubs, widely used for ground cover. There are many other species and varieties, and the deciduous ones are grown principally for their wonderfully rich autumn colours and distinctive fruits, which follow the somewhat inconspicuous flowers.

Popular species and varieties

The two best known forms are cultivars of the evergreen *E. fortunei*, a native of Japan. 'Emerald 'n' Gold' (AGM) is noted for its green, gold and pink leaves. 'Silver Queen' (AGM) has foliage attractively edged with white.

One that can be relied upon to provide a colourful autumn show is *E. europaeus* 'Red Cascade' (AGM), for not only do the leaves have rich autumn colours, but the plentiful, large, rosy-red seed capsules are attractive in their own right. It is a good idea to grow several together, as this will ensure cross-pollination.

Cultivation

Soil type *Euonymus* grows happily in most good garden soils.
Planting These shrubs will grow in sun or light shade. The evergreen species and varieties should be grown in a spot where they are not subjected to icy winds. Planting can be done in autumn or spring.
Pruning Not generally required. Any straggly growth on the deciduous species can be cut out in early spring to retain a good shape.
Propagation Cuttings of around 7cm (3in) in length, taken with a heel, in mid to late summer.
Pests and diseases Aphids can attack the deciduous species, and these should be promptly dealt with by insecticide.

PLANT DIRECTORY

ABOVE *Exochorda* x *macrantha* 'The Bride' makes a splendid site when in full bloom

27. EXOCHORDA

Common name Pearl bush
Family Rosaceae

This is a small genus comprising four species of deciduous shrubs with white flowers. They are native to the Far East where they are to be found in tightly wooded areas.

Popular species and varieties

One exochorda that is widely available is *E. giraldii* var. *wilsonii*, a free-flowering, upright-growing shrub that reaches 3m (10ft) in height. In late spring it produces racemes of white flowers up to 5cm (2in) across.

The best known cultivar is unquestionably *E.* x *macrantha* 'The Bride' (AGM). This forms a lax, arching shrub up to 1.8m (5ft) in height. In spring the racemes of pure white flowers appear.

Cultivation

Soil type Most good, well-drained but moist soils, with the exception of shallow chalky types.
Planting Plant in the autumn or spring, choosing a sunny or lightly shaded spot.
Maintenance Cut out, after flowering, any weak or straggly growth.
Propagation Softwood cuttings can be taken in the summer.
Pests and diseases Normally trouble free.

GARDENING WITH SHRUBS

28. FORSYTHIA

Common name Golden bell bush
Family Oleaceae

Spring would not be the same without the very popular and colourful forsythia which produces masses of blooms on leafless branches. Easily grown, it has much to offer after the long dreary winter months.

Popular species and varieties

There are several species of these colourful shrubs, ranging from those of dwarf habit which grow to around 60cm (24in), to the taller varieties reaching 4m (12ft) or more. Flower colour varies from light primrose to rich golden yellow. Among the best known are the ones listed under *F. x intermedia*. Well to the fore is 'Lynwood' (AGM) with its rich yellow blooms. Two others are 'Arnold Grant', not so free-flowering, but with larger, pendant blooms, and 'Spectabilis', an old favourite, with narrow, twisted golden-yellow petals.

Forsythia suspensa (AGM) is an arching shrub with mid-green leaves. The clusters of bell-shaped blooms appear in early spring. This is a good subject to train up a wall. There are some varieties with dark stems – two are 'Nyman's' with reddish-purple stems and *F. suspensa atrocaulis*, almost black.

The dwarf forsythias are good early flowering shrubs for the front of a border or large rock garden. *F. viridissima* 'Bronxensis' grows to just 30cm (12in), and has yellow flowers in early spring.

Cultivation

Soil type Most good, moist, well-drained garden soils.
Planting In either the autumn or spring. Choose a sunny or lightly shaded spot.
Maintenance Prune forsythias immediately after flowering. Cut back about one-third of the oldest branches that have flowered.
Propagation Cuttings root very successfully. Semi-ripe cuttings with a heel should be taken in late summer, or opt instead for softwood cuttings in late spring.
Pests and diseases Normally no problems, although birds can sometimes pull off flower buds.

LEFT *Forsythia* x *intermedia* 'Spectabilis'

29. FUCHSIA (HARDY)

Common name none
Family Onagraceae

In mild districts the hardy fuchsias often come through the winter unscathed, and can reach 2m (6ft) or more in height. In others, the stems can be killed by frost. This is not normally a problem, however, as in the spring they invariably produce new growth from the base.

Popular species and varieties

It is important to choose those that are regarded as hardy. One of the best known is *F. magellanica*. The straight species is available, although many choose one of the named varieties. The flowers of this shrub are slender and freely produced in mid to late summer. Among those to look out for are *F. magellanica* var. *gracillis* (AGM), with small rosy purple flowers, and the hybrid 'Madame Cornelissen', with red and white blooms. Also well worth considering are the golden-leaved 'Aurea', the equally attractive variegated form 'Variegata' (AGM), and 'Versicolor' (AGM), its leaves edged with white and cream.

There are numerous hybrids suitable for the garden. 'Lady Thumb' (AGM) has semi-double flowers with pink sepals and white petals, and grows to just 45cm (18in). Even smaller is 'Tom Thumb' (AGM) with red and violet blooms on sturdy plants just over 35cm (14in) high. An old stager, still as popular as ever, is 'Mrs Popple' (AGM), vigorous with red and purple flowers.

Cultivation

Soil type Most humus-rich, moist, well-drained soils.
Planting Best carried out in the spring, as rising soil temperatures will help plants to establish quickly. They can be grown in sun or light shade.
Maintenance Apart from those growing in mild districts, the stems should be cut back to just above ground level, in early spring. Deeply mulch around the bases of the plants with peat, or other suitable material, in the autumn.
Propagation Softwood cuttings of around 7cm (3in) in length can be taken in early summer.
Pests and diseases The hardy fuchsias are generally trouble free. Aphids can be a problem on new growth; spray with insecticide as soon as seen.

ABOVE One of the best hardy fuchsias is *F. magellanica* 'Versicolor'

ABOVE *Garrya elliptica* is a shrub that flowers in the depths of winter

30. GARRYA

Common name Silk tassel bush
Family Garryaceae

Only one species of this shrub is in general cultivation, and is grown for its display of catkins in late winter.

Popular species and varieties

Garrya elliptica is a native of the west coast of America, particularly California and Oregon, growing to around 3m (10ft) in height, with thick, leathery leaves. The catkins are freely produced, at first grey-green, then changing to a dull cream as they age. 'James Roof' (AGM) is the one to look out for, as its catkins are thicker, and longer at 35cm (14in) in length.

Cultivation

Soil type Moist, humus-rich, well-drained soils.
Planting Plant in early spring. Choose a sheltered spot in sun or light shade where the plant will not be subjected to cold winds (ideally where it will have the protection of a south facing-wall). Garrya resents root disturbance, so choose a sturdy young plant and set it out in a place where it will remain.
Maintenance Regular pruning is not required. Any dead or straggly branches can be removed in the spring.
Pests and diseases Usually unaffected. Blackening or blotches on leaves is a sign of frost damage.

PLANT DIRECTORY

ABOVE *Genista* – a free-flowering compact shrub

31. GENISTA

Common name **Broom**
Family **Papilionaceae**

These sun-loving shrubs in the pea and bean family are particularly noted for their very free-flowering habits. Many forms are ideal subjects for ground cover and for use on dry banks or low walls, while others make excellent specimen plants.

Popular species and varieties

One of the best known members of the family is Spanish gorse (*Genista hispanica*). Growing to 60cm (24in), it covers itself with bright golden-yellow flowers in late spring and early summer. It has prickly foliage, so should be positioned with care.

Equally popular is *G. lydia* (AGM), which forms a neat shrub of a similar size. Flowering is from mid-spring to late spring; here again the foliage disappears under a profusion of bright yellow flowers. One genista that has a vigorous habit, growing to 3m (10ft) or more, is *G. tenera* 'Golden Shower' (AGM).

Cultivation

Soil type These shrubs are best in poor, light, sandy soil. Rich conditions can reduce flowering.
Planting Choose an open, sunny spot. Genistas resent root disturbance. Choose sturdy young plants, and set them out in the autumn or spring.
Maintenance There is little required in the way of maintenance. Pruning is not necessary. Any long, straggly branches can be cut back after flowering. Take care not to cut into old wood.
Propagation Semi-ripe cuttings of about 7cm (3in) in length, with a heel, can be taken in mid-summer.
Pests and diseases Generally trouble free.

ABOVE *Halimium* 'Susan' – given a well-drained spot it will cover itself with flowers

32. HALIMIUM

Common name None
Family Cistaceae

These shrubs originate from the Mediterranean region and are closely related to *Cistus* and *Helianthemum*. They have a dwarf habit, making them ideal candidates for the front of a flower border or perhaps on a large rock garden.

Popular species and varieties

The most popular is *H. ocymoides* (AGM), which has a free-flowering habit, growing to around 60cm (24in). The leaves are narrow and grey-green. The early summer bright yellow blooms, each 2.5cm (1in) across, have distinctive chocolate blotches at the base of the petals. 'Susan' (AGM) has a more compact habit, with slightly larger leaves and the same handsome flowers.

Another species that is hardy in mild districts is *H. lasianthum* (AGM). This grows to 90cm (36in) in height, and produces golden-yellow flowers with a purple-brown blotch. 'Concolor' is very similar, the clear yellow flowers lacking the blotches.

Cultivation

Soil type Prefers a good, but light soil.
Planting Choose a sunny spot in a sheltered position. Set out in the autumn or spring.
Propagation Cuttings around 7cm (3in), with a heel, should be taken in early to mid-summer.
Maintenance No pruning required.
Pests and diseases Usually no problems.

ABOVE **Witch hazels, of which there are many forms, flower in the coldest months**

33. HAMAMELIS

Common name Witch hazel
Family Hamamelidaceae

The witch hazels are grown principally for their winter flowers, adding colour to the garden at a particularly bleak time. Some take on good autumn colour before the leaves fall. Flowers are produced in clusters held on leafless branches, and have a rather strange spidery appearance.

Popular species and varieties

Many of those grown are varieties of *H. x intermedia*. Among them are 'Arnold Promise' (AGM), with large yellow flowers in mid-winter; 'Diane' (AGM), a deep bronzy-red; 'Orange Beauty' a deep rich yellow, and 'Jelena' (AGM), sometimes listed as 'Copper Beauty', with very attractive coppery-orange flowers.

The Chinese witch hazel (*Hamamelis mollis*) (AGM) flowers at the same time. This forms a neat shrub with soft, slightly hairy leaves. The flowers are golden yellow and fragrant. There are a number of named varieties: 'Goldcrest' is a good choice; its flowers slightly later. The rich golden-yellow blooms are tinged with red at their base. The foliage turns yellow in the autumn.

Cultivation

Soil type Neutral or acid soils are best, especially those that are moisture-retentive. The structure of heavy soils should be improved by incorporating some peat, leaf mould or well-rotted manure at planting time.
Planting Choose a sunny, sheltered spot. Plant in autumn or spring.
Maintenance Pruning is not required. Any straggly branches growing on mature specimens can be cut back after flowering.
Propagation Long shoots are flexible, and can be layered in late summer. Cuttings of around 10cm (4in) in length, with a heel, can be taken in late summer. They are slow and difficult to root.
Pests and diseases Usually no problems are experienced with witch hazels.

GARDENING WITH **SHRUBS**

PLANT DIRECTORY

34. HEBE

Common name Shrubby veronica
Family Scrophulariaceae

This group of evergreen shrubs is native to New Zealand, and for many years was included in the genus *Veronica*, hence the common name. Hebes are fairly short-lived, and vary considerably in hardiness. These are plants for mild districts where they are not subjected to cold winds. They are accommodating plants, and will grow in smoky or salt-laden atmospheres.

Numerous varieties are offered in garden centres, some with broad leaves and others that have tight, scale-like leaves resembling a whipcord. As a general rule, the larger the individual leaves are on a *Hebe*, the more likely the plant will be damaged – or even killed – by severe frost.

Hebes are easily recognized by their bottle-brush flower spikes usually produced in large numbers. They vary in size from bushes of 3m (10ft) or more, down to ground-hugging varieties, ideal for the front of a border or a rock garden.

Popular species and varieties

There are a great number of species and varieties available. Among them is *Hebe salicifolia*, which produces white-tinged-lilac flowerspikes on 3m (10ft) high bushes from late spring until late summer. *H. macrantha* (AGM) is not one of the hardiest and requires a warm spot, but it is a good rock garden shrub as it grows to just 60cm (24in); it also has white flowers.

Another popular dwarf variety is 'Baby Marie', one of the first to flower. Growing to just 20cm (8in), it has reddish brown stems and pale lilac flowers. 'Caledonia', with striking violet blooms each with a white eye, grows taller and reaches 45cm (18in). It has a long flowering period.

H. ochracea 'James Stirling' (AGM) is very different. One of the whipcord types it is grown for its golden foliage. The white flowers are sparsely produced and then only on mature specimens, which never exceed 45cm (18in). This is a good plant to provide colour during the dull winter months.

Two bushy shrubs worth considering are 'Autumn Glory', with masses of violet-blue spikes, and 'Great Orme' (AGM), bright pink. Both bloom for many weeks during the summer months.

Cultivation

Soil type Most types of well-drained soil.
Planting Hebes are sun lovers so choose an open spot, but remember to check on hardiness. Planting can be done in the autumn or spring. The latter will enable plants to establish quickly as soil temperatures rise.
Pruning Not required. Should you need to cut back any branches, this can be done in the spring, but avoid cutting into old wood. Dead-heading will prolong the display of flowers.
Propagation Semi-ripe cuttings of non-flowering shoots may be taken in summer.
Pests and diseases Very few problems.

LEFT **The low-growing *Hebe* 'Caledonia'**

GARDENING WITH **SHRUBS**

ABOVE *Helianthemum* 'Rhodanthe Carneum'

35. HELIANTHEMUM

Common name Rock rose
Family Cistaceae

Among my lasting garden memories is a sunny early summer morning and coming across a large rock bank planted entirely with helianthemums, widely known as rock roses. The numerous plants provided a fantastic kaleidoscope of colour. Helianthemums are no strangers to our gardens, and are currently enjoying a well-deserved surge in popularity. These are easy-to-grow shrubs and will thrive in even quite poor soil conditions. They are ideal for an open pocket on the rock garden or for edging the border.

Those most widely available are hybrids with single or double flowers. There is considerable variation in both leaf and flower colour, the latter including crimson, pink, flame, a lovely coppery orange, bright yellow and white. Individual blooms last for only one day but there is no need to worry as next morning new flowers will open. This goes on for several weeks. The singles retain their petals for a longer time than the doubles.

Popular species and varieties

In any list of helianthemums you will come across varieties with the 'Ben' prefix. These are old stagers having stood the test of time well. Among the most popular is 'Ben Fhada', its yellow, orange-centred flowers contrast well against the dark green foliage. 'Ben Hacklar' is a vigorous plant with large copper-orange blooms over rich green leaves. 'Ben Ledi' has narrow leaves and flowers of a deep wine red. One not to overlook in this series is 'Ben Nevis' with a plentiful supply of tawny orange-yellow flowers.

The Royal Horticultural Society's Award of Garden Merit is currently held by seven varieties. One of these is 'Fire Dragon', with vivid orange-red flowers over grey-green foliage. Others holding this award include 'Amy Baring', noted for its profusion of rich golden yellow blooms, and 'Henfield Brilliant', a spreading plant that, in late spring and early summer, is almost hidden beneath a mass of eye-catching flowers in vivid brick red.

Two others with single blooms are 'Rhodanthe Carneum', which can sometimes still be found listed under its old name of 'Wisley Pink'. An old favourite, 'Wisley Primrose' is a spreading shrub with grey-green foliage and masses of lovely pale primrose flowers.

Two award holders with double blooms are 'Jubilee' which produces a fine show of sulphur-yellow flowers, and the equally attractive brick-red 'Mrs. C. W. Earle', the blooms of which are held clear of the dark green leaves.

'Coppernob' has deep orange blooms, each with a dark red centre. Another that should not be overlooked is 'Wisley White' with masses of single blooms. Look out also for 'The Bride'; its flowers have a rather interesting white papery texture.

For those who like something different then 'Raspberry Ripple' with cream and dark pink flowers is worth considering. 'Chocolate Blotch' is also popular, the buff-coloured blooms have a distinctive chocolate brown blotch at the base of the petals. One with a low-growing habit, reaching just 20cm (8in) in height, is 'Fireball' with lovely dark red flowers contrasting well against the foliage.

Cultivation

Soil type Light, well-drained, rather poor soils.
Planting These are sun lovers, and if planted in full sun they will flower profusely. Plant in the autumn or spring. Allow plenty of space as some varieties spread to 60–90cm (24–36in). Choose a selection of colours if planting on a bank, or alternatively select just one variety, which will have a very dramatic effect.
Maintenance When flowering has finished trim the plants with a pair of shears; this will keep them tidy, encourage new growth, and often a further flush of flowers later in the season.
Propagation Helianthemums are not long-living plants so it is a good plan to keep youngsters coming along. Increase stock by taking cuttings with a heel in early or mid-summer. Take the material from non-flowering shoots.
Pests and diseases Generally, these shrubs are not troubled by pests. A fungal disease can cause stems to collapse. In bad cases lift and burn the affected plants.

GARDENING WITH **SHRUBS**

PLANT DIRECTORY

36. HIBISCUS

Common name Shrubby mallow
Family Malvaceae

One of the main features of these shrubs is their free-flowering habit. They are available in a wide range of colours with both single and double blooms. Flowering usually commences in early summer and extends on into autumn. *Hibiscus* are sun lovers, and are not difficult provided they have a free-draining fertile soil with shelter from cold winds.

Popular species and varieties

Hibiscus syriacus is, not surprisingly, a native of Syria. This deciduous well-branched shrub grows to 2m (6ft) or more in height. There are numerous named forms available. One which is certainly high on the list for popularity is 'Blue Bird', or now more correctly 'Oiseau Bleu' (AGM). Its single mid-blue blooms with a dark red centre are 7.5cm (3in) across.

'Red Heart' is another eye-catching variety, its large white flowers having a distinctive red eye. Anyone who enjoys pink blooms should find 'Pink Giant' to their liking. This is another with single flowers. 'Russian Violet' is a rich dark violet, 'Hambo' (AGM) is a blush-white with crimson centre, while 'Woodbridge' (AGM) is a popular variety: a rich rose pink with a deeper centre.

Among the double-flowered forms are 'Jeanne d'Arc' with white blooms, and 'Lady Stanley', a blush pink with maroon centre, which has been in cultivation for well over 100 years.

Cultivation

Soil type Humus-rich, well-drained soils.
Planting Choose a sunny spot where the plants will be sheltered from cold winds. Hibiscus can be slow to establish, and they always flower best in hot summers. Planting can be carried out in the autumn or spring. In cold districts the latter is preferable.
Maintenance Pruning is not generally required. Any long or straggly shoots can be cut back immediately after flowering.
Propagation Cuttings of around 7.5cm (3in) long, with a heel, taken from half-ripe, non-flowering shoots in early summer.
Pests and diseases Aphids can become a nuisance – if seen treat as soon as possible with insecticide.

LEFT *Hibiscus syriacus* 'Oiseau Bleu' flowers from mid-summer onwards

GARDENING WITH **SHRUBS**

PLANT DIRECTORY

37. HYDRANGEA

Common name None
Family Hydrangeaceae

These are very popular shrubs grown principally for their large showy flowers. There are several types: the common 'Mopheads' and equally attractive 'Lacecaps', together with others of upright or climbing habit.

Popular species and varieties

There are many 'Mophead' varieties (Hortensias), so which you grow is a matter of personal choice. One with a rather formidable name is 'Generale Vicomptesse de Vibraye' (AGM), noted for its early, free-flowering habit. The flowers are pale blue or pink. 'Niedersachsen' follows close behind, a vigorous grower. 'Deutschland' is a rich pink or light blue.

Many have blue flowers when grown in acid conditions, and are pink when grown in alkaline soils. The whites are unaffected, remaining constant especially when grown in light shade; they will take on a reddish tinge if planted in a sunny spot.

'Lacecap' varieties to look out for are 'Blue Wave' (AGM) and the lovely white 'Lanarth', which has neat, compact growth.

The climbing hydrangea is *H. petiolaris* (AGM), a vigorous self-clinging deciduous shrub which can, in ideal conditions, reach 20m (60ft) or more, producing flattened clusters of white flowers in late spring. It is no stranger to Western gardens having been introduced from the Far East in 1865.

One more species is the oak leaf hydrangea (*H. quercifolia*) (AGM). This produces long white flowers, at first creamy-white, taking on a pinkish tinge as they age. The US-bred 'Snow Queen' is the one to look for; a large-flowered choice with upright panicles over bushy growth.

Cultivation

Soil type Humus-rich, well-drained soil. As already seen, soil conditions affect the flower colour.
Planting Select a sheltered position in a lightly shaded spot. Avoid areas where there is early morning sun after late frost as this can damage new growth. Plant in the autumn or spring. The climbing hydrangea can take two or three years to become established.
Maintenance Pruning is not required. Flowers of 'Mophead' hydrangeas should not be removed until late winter. Not only are they still attractive in the winter months, but they also provide shelter for new, young growth. In the case of 'Lacecaps', remove the dead-heads immediately after flowering. If you wish to cut back any straggly branches, this should also be done in late winter.
Propagation Semi-ripe cuttings of around 15cm (6in) in length, taken from non-flowering shoots.
Pests and diseases Aphids can attack young growth in the spring.

LEFT **Leave flowers on hydrangeas throughout winter – they will protect the buds**

GARDENING WITH SHRUBS

ABOVE **Most forms of *Hypericum* can be used for brightening up dull parts of the garden**

38. HYPERICUM

Common name St John's wort
Family Clusiaceae

Members of the *Hypericum* genus are easy-to-grow, undemanding shrubs that can be relied upon to brighten up dull spots in the garden. The best known and most widely available is the rose of Sharon (*Hypericum calycinum*), which will thrive in numerous difficult positions – under trees or on dry banks, it does not seem to matter. It is a vigorous grower, and ideal for providing ground cover. But it can become a nuisance.

Popular species and varieties

H. calycinum produces large golden flowers with conspicuous stamens, from late spring to early autumn, over dense growth of 45cm (18in) in height.

There are a considerable number of alternative species, including *H. kouytchense* (AGM). This has upright growth and deep yellow flowers with very long stamens, carried in early and mid-summer. They are followed by red seed capsules.

One hypericum that is very popular is 'Hidcote' (AGM), producing a long succession of rich golden blooms on neat, 1.2m (4ft) high bushes, from late spring until late summer.

Cultivation

Soil type Any non-waterlogged garden soil.
Planting This can be carried out in the autumn or spring, in open, sunny or lightly shaded areas.
Pruning In late winter, every few years, *H. calycinum* should be cut back hard. This will keep it compact. At other times trim to keep it in shape.
Propagation Semi-ripe cuttings with a heel, taken from non-flowering shoots in the summer.
Pests and diseases Generally trouble free, although *H. calycinum* can be attacked by rust.

ABOVE *Ilex aquifolium* 'Silver Queen' is an attractive holly with variegated foliage

39. ILEX

Common name Holly
Family Aquifoliaceae

Prickly leaves and Christmas decorations – these are the two things that immediately come to mind when holly is mentioned. This large genus has much to offer, with hollies having all shades of green and variegated leaves. Many hollies have red berries, whilst others offer yellow or black. There are a few deciduous forms, but most are evergreen, and there are even forms with spineless leaves.

Popular species and varieties

There are forms of *Ilex* available for all sizes of garden. The most commonly grown is *Ilex aquifolium* (AGM), and its numerous varieties and cultivars which can be very different in growth habit, shape and colour of leaves and berries. They are grown, it has to be said, for their foliage and berries: the flowers are insignificant.

The berries, which last throughout winter, are carried only on female plants, so it is important that a male is nearby in order to cross-pollinate. Take time to look up a variety before buying, as names can be misleading. 'Golden Queen', for instance, is a male form. It is an eye-catching variety; the broad dark green leaves have a wide yellow margin.

Also with gold margins, on almost spineless leaves, is 'Golden van Tol' (female). 'Silver Queen' (male) has cream-edged leaves. 'J. C. van Tol' (AGM) (female) has almost spineless leaves and is noted for its bright red berries. Another good variety is the golden hedgehog holly (*I. aquifolium* 'Ferrox Argentea') (AGM), male. This is a medium-sized shrub with creamy white spines to its leaves.

Cultivation

Soil type Any good well-drained soil.
Planting Sun or light shade, with a sunny spot for those with variegated foliage. Planting can be done in the autumn or spring.
Pruning No regular pruning is required. Any specimen shrubs can be trimmed to shape in early summer. When used as hedging, trim annually in early spring. Variegated hollies can, on occasions, produce green shoots; when seen cut these back immediately.
Propagation Take 7cm (3in) long cuttings with a heel in mid-summer. Select well-ripened current year's growth. Alternatively, layer shrubs in early autumn, eventually separating the plants two years later.
Pests and diseases Holly leaf miner can be a problem. The larvae tunnel into the leaves. If only a few leaves are affected take them off and burn them. Insecticide will kill the adult insects, but the larvae are more difficult – a systemic insecticide may be effective.

ABOVE A newly planted *Kalmia latifolia* can take time to settle down

40. KALMIA

Common name Calico bush
Family Ericaceae

Acid soil conditions are essential to grow these attractive shrubs. There are eight species, with *Kalmia latifolia* and its forms the most widely grown.

Popular species and varieties

The mountain laurel (*Kalmia latifolia*) (AGM) grows to around 1.8m (5ft) in height. It has glossy foliage, similar in many ways to that of rhododendron. The 15cm (6in) long clusters of flowers appear in late spring. Of the varieties, 'Ostbo Red' (AGM) is a good choice, its bright red buds open to pale pink. 'Olympic Fire' has large pink flowers. Others to look for include 'Minuet', possessing a dwarf habit and offering maroon flowers; 'Alpine Pink', pink buds open to reveal pink and white flowers, and 'Bullseye', reddish foliage and bronze-red blooms.

Cultivation

Soil type Moist, acid soil.
Planting Choose a lightly shaded spot; plant in the autumn or spring.
Maintenance Pruning is not required. Remove the dead flower clusters.
Propagation Cuttings of around 7cm (3in), taken from semi-ripe wood in mid-summer. Kalmias can also be layered.
Pests and diseases Generally trouble free.

PLANT DIRECTORY

ABOVE *Kerria japonica* – easily grown and noted for its masses of golden-yellow flowers in spring

41. KERRIA

Common name Jew's mallow
Family Rosaceae

Few early spring-flowering shrubs can equal the display produced by *Kerria japonica* 'Pleniflora' (AGM) which comes into all its glory just as the forsythia is beginning to fade.

Popular species and varieties

Kerria japonica was introduced to our gardens from its native China in 1804, and it soon became very popular. Today, Kerria is commonly seen in gardens everywhere. The most popular is the yellow, double-flowered *Kerria japonica* 'Pleniflora' (AGM). Growing up to 2m (6ft), it covers itself with blooms in late winter and early spring. The larger-flowered 'Golden Guinea' (AGM) is another splendid shrub with single, bright golden-yellow blooms. Look also for 'Picta', listed for many years as 'Variegata', with silver variegated foliage and single yellow flowers. This variety grows to 1.5m (5ft) and has a more spreading habit.

Cultivation

Soil type Any good humus-rich, well-drained soil.
Planting Kerrias are happy in sun or light shade; the latter is recommended to stop flowers bleaching. Autumn and spring are suitable times to plant.
Pruning After flowering has finished, cut the stems back to strong new growth lower down. A few of the oldest branches can be cut back to ground level, which will encourage new growth.
Propagation Kerrias often produce rooted suckers, which can be carefully detached to provide new plants. Alternatively, take semi-ripe cuttings with a heel in mid to late summer.
Pests and diseases Generally trouble free.

ABOVE *Lavandula angustifolia* 'Rosea' is a good choice to grow alongside other varieties

42. LAVANDULA

Common name Lavender
Family Lamiaceae

These are among the best known of all shrubs, and are particularly valued for their aromatic foliage and flowers.

Popular species and varieties

Among the most popular is the old English lavender (*Lavandula angustifolia*), with pale blue flowers on long stems. Originating from Mediterranean regions, it has been grown in the UK since the middle of the 16th century. There is also a white form listed as 'Alba', and a whole host of varieties, mostly hybrids. Among these is the ever-popular 'Hidcote' (AGM), with violet flowers growing to 45cm (18in). The pink-flowered 'Hidcote Pink' is also worth considering.

One to look for, with a lower growing habit, is 'Nana Alba'. Ideal for edging, it grows to just 30cm (12in). For a change try 'Rosea', its pink blooms reaching 45cm (18in). 'Twickel Purple' (AGM) is a compact form with broad leaves and blue flowers.

In recent years French lavender (*L. stoechas*) (AGM) has become very popular. This is different in that its dark purple blooms are borne in dense, congested heads topped by distinctive terminal bracts. It has been grown here for a great many years and requires a warm, dry, sunny spot.

Cultivation

Soil type Well-drained, humus-rich soil is suitable.
Planting Choose a sunny spot, and plant in either autumn or spring. If planting a lavender 'hedge', set the plants 22–30cm (9–12in) apart.
Pruning Remove dead flowers and stalks after flowering has finished; lightly trim in late summer. In early spring trim back old, straggly plants to promote new bushy growth from the base. This is also the time to trim established hedges into shape.
Propagation Semi-ripe cuttings taken with a heel, in mid-summer.
Pests and diseases Froghoppers can inhabit the plants. With their familiar protective 'cuckoo spit' coating, they can spoil the appearance of the plant. Pick them off or spray with insecticide.

43. LIGUSTRUM

Common name Privet
Family Oleaceae

Numerous shrubs are used as hedges, among them common privet (*Ligustrum vulgare*), a great favourite for years, especially in town front gardens. Privet has the ability to grow in shady spots, and appears to be unaffected by polluted air. If regularly trimmed, the bushes seldom flower.

This group of shrubs has much to offer, both evergreen and deciduous forms, and when they flower, the blooms are white and often fragrant.

Popular species and varieties

One of the best for producing a show of blooms is *Ligustrum quihoui* (AGM), a deciduous shrub growing to around 2.4m (8ft) high. From mid to late summer the 30cm (12in) long cones of small, white flowers are carred on stiff branches. *Ligustrum tschonoskii* 'Vicaryi' is another good choice. This is an evergreen shrub noted for its rich bronzy-purple winter colour.

Others to look for are the Japanese privet (*L. japonicum*), growing to 2m (6ft), with evergreen leaves similar to those of a camellia, and white late summer flowers. *L. japonicum* 'Rotundifolium' is a low-growing, compact form with leathery dark green leaves. The common privet (*L. vulgare*) is still widely available, but is not used as often these days for hedging.

Cultivation

Soil type Any fertile garden soil.
Planting Privets will grow in sunny or lightly shaded positions. They can be planted in the autumn or spring. Those grown for hedging should be spaced 45cm (18in) apart. Cut back at planting time (or the following spring, if planting in autumn) to promote strong, bushy plants.
Pruning This is only necessary for those grown as hedging; clip in early spring and again in late summer.
Propagation Semi-ripe cuttings with a heel may be taken in summer. Hardwood cuttings of some varieties can be taken in late autumn. Root these in a nursery bed.
Pests and diseases Leaf miner and thrips can attack.

ABOVE The foliage of *Ligustrum tschonoskii* 'Vicaryi' turns to bronze-purple in winter

GARDENING WITH **SHRUBS**

PLANT DIRECTORY

44. LONICERA

Common name Honeysuckle
Family Caprifoliaceae

One of our most fragrant plants, the common honeysuckle (*Lonicera periclymenum*) is often seen in hedgerows, and is a popular garden plant. Honeysuckles are divided into two groups: the better-known climbers, and those with a shrubby habit.

Popular species and varieties

There are many from which to choose. *Lonicera nitida* is grown for its small, round and dense foliage – ideal for low hedging. The flowers are insignificant. 'Baggesen's Gold' has golden-yellow leaves, and 'Ernest Wilson' is noted for its slightly arching habit.

One species that has been in cultivation for over 250 years is *L. tatarica*. This is a vigorous deciduous shrub that can grow to 3m (10ft) or more in height. The masses of pink flowers are produced in mid to late spring, and are followed by red berries. 'Arnold's Red' has deep purple-red blooms with larger berries; it often has a second flush of flowers in the autumn.

The climbing honeysuckles include *L. periclymenum* 'Graham Thomas' (AGM) with heavily scented cream flowers, and *L. x brownii* 'Dropmore Scarlet', a deciduous plant with a long period of flower.

Cultivation

Soil type Honeysuckles require moist, humus-rich soil.
Planting All forms can be planted in autumn or spring, but the evergreen climbers are best planted in the spring. Honeysuckles are happy in full sun or light shade.
Pruning It is advisable to thin out old wood from time to time after flowering, which will encourage new growth.
Propagation Semi-ripe cuttings taken in early to mid-summer. Honeysuckles can also be layered, severing from the parent plant a year later.
Pests and diseases Aphids might attack new growth and flowers; as soon as they are seen, spray with a suitable insecticide. Powdery mildew can attack; spray with a fungicide immediately.

LEFT *Lonicera nitida* 'Baggesen's Gold'

GARDENING WITH **SHRUBS**

PLANT DIRECTORY

45. MAGNOLIA

Common name none
Family Magnoliaceae

One has just to see magnolias in full bloom to appreciate that they are truly among the most beautiful of all shrubs. Ancestors of the magnolias we grow today lived on earth during the Cretaceous period, making them some of the first flowering plants.

Of the garden forms of this large group of flowering trees and shrubs, two members in particular add a great deal to the scene in spring. *Magnolia stellata* (AGM) produces white, star-shaped blooms, and another great favourite, *M. x. soulangeana*, has large, goblet-shaped flowers.

Popular species and varieties

One of the best species for the smaller garden is the star magnolia (*M. stellata*) (AGM). It is a slow-growing, rounded shrub that seldom exceeds 3m (10ft) in height. In mid-spring the hairy buds open to reveal the pure white, numerous-petalled flowers. It is no stranger to our gardens, having been introduced from Japan in 1862. There are a number of selected cultivars available, among which is 'Waterlily' (AGM), with broad petals, and the free-flowering 'Royal Star'.

Another great favourite, *M. x soulangeana*, is a hybrid of *M. denudata* and *M. lilliflora*, originating from France in 1820, and now found in gardens worldwide. It is among the easiest to grow, being very hardy. Position with care as it will grow into a tree-like structure, covering itself with pale to deep pink, goblet-shaped blooms in early spring. There are many cultivars, ranging from pure white to a rich deep purple; all have a slight fragrance. Flowers appear before the leaves.

There are also many hybrid magnolias available, such as 'Vulcan', a brilliant ruby-red raised in New Zealand. The bright pink 'Star Wars' is another good choice.

Cultivation

Soil type Good, fertile soils are preferred. Check before purchase, as some magnolias do not like alkaline soils.
Planting This is best carried out in spring. Magnolias are happy in sun or light shade. Choose a spot where they are not subjected to cold winds.
Pruning Any unwanted shoots or branches should be removed after flowering.
Propagation Layer in late winter or early spring. It will usually take two years before rooting takes place. Alternatively, try taking 10cm (4in) long cuttings of half-ripened shoots with a heel, in early summer. Magnolias are difficult to root.
Pests and diseases It is most unlikely that pests will be a problem. However, frost can damage buds, causing them to turn brown, and buds can sometimes be attacked by grey- mould fungus disease.

LEFT *Magnolia stellata* 'Royal Star' produces masses of white flowers in early spring

ABOVE *Olearia cheesemanii* – sun-lovers that require a sheltered place in the garden

46. OLEARIA

Common name Daisy bush
Family Asteraceae

These free-flowering shrubs almost completely cover themselves with clusters of daisy-like flowers in summer, hence their common name. They are splendid subjects for coastal areas, coping well with salt-laden atmospheres. These are sun lovers, but not all are reliably hardy.

Popular species and varieties

One that has a good reputation for hardiness is *Olearia x haastii*. This grows to 1.5m (5ft) in height and has a free-flowering habit; the white flowers are held well clear of the box-like foliage.

With yellow foliage, *O. nummularifolia* has slightly smaller flower heads. Meanwhile, *O. cheesemanii* has leaves with wavy edges and, here again, masses of white flowers. This is one for a sheltered spot in a mild district.

Cultivation

Soil type Any good fertile, well-drained soil.
Planting Choose a sunny spot. Planting can be carried out in autumn or spring.
Pruning General pruning is not required, but it is advisable to trim over with shears at the end of summer to remove dead flowers. Any stray shoots can be removed in early spring.
Propagation Semi-ripe cuttings, taken in early spring.
Pests and diseases Generally trouble free.

47. OSMANTHUS

Common name none
Family Oleaceae

These attractive evergreen shrubs have a neat, rounded habit, some with holly-like leaves. The majority bloom in the spring but there are some autumn-flowering varieties. They are happy in most garden soils.

Popular species and varieties

One of the best known is *Osmanthus* x *burkwoodii* (AGM), a neat bush not exceeding 3m (10ft) in height, with tough oval dark green toothed leaves. The fragrant white flowers are freely produced and appear in the spring. Another first-class form is *O. delavayi* (AGM), which has a slow-growing habit, in time reaching 2m (6ft). The small fragrant white flowers are produced in mid-spring.

Among the autumn-flowering species is *O. heterophyllus* with bright, holly-like leaves. In late summer and early autumn it produces sweetly scented white flowers. It is a good choice for a hedge. Equally attractive is *O. heterophyllus* 'Aureomarginatus', the leaves of which are edged with yellow.

Cultivation

Soil type Most humus-rich, well-drained types.
Planting Osmanthus are best grown in lightly shaded places, although they will perform reasonably well in full sun. Avoid places where they would be subjected to cold winds.
Maintenance Pruning is not required. Any growth that has become leggy can be cut back immediately after flowering. If *O. heterophyllus* is grown as a hedge, trim it in early spring.
Propagation Take cuttings from half-ripe wood, around 10cm (4in) long, in the summer. Alternatively, layer the shrub in the autumn.
Pests and diseases Generally trouble free.

RIGHT *Osmanthus* x *burkwoodii* is a splendid shrub with dark glossy leaves and fragrant flowers

ABOVE *Paeonia suffruticosa*, originally grown in China

48. PAEONIA

Common name Tree peony
Family Paeoniaceae

These are among the most attractive of all flowering shrubs and are not to be confused with their cousins grown in herbaceous borders. The tree peonies are attractive both in leaf and flower; they are hardy, but young growth can be damaged by late frosts. Over recent years many splendid varieties in a wide range of colours have been imported from China.

Popular species and varieties

The best known is the mountain peony (*P. suffruticosa*), with large blooms 15cm (6in) across. There are many varieties, and among recent introductions are 'Dark Black Purple' (also known as 'Sheng Hei Zi'), a striking double-flowered purple; 'Pink Lady' ('Fen Qiao') with very large frilly double pink blooms, and 'White Jade' ('Bai Yu'), a lovely double white.

Among the best of the yellow tree peonies is *P. lutea* var. *ludlowii* (AGM) with large golden-yellow flowers. A final one to look for is *P. rockii*, with large white blooms that are highlighted by a maroon blotch at the base of each petal.

Cultivation

Soil type Most well-drained fertile soils, except poor sandy conditions and waterlogged clay.
Planting Choose a sunny but sheltered spot. It may be necessary to protect the young growth against late frosts. The best time to plant is in the spring.
Pruning Generally no pruning is required. Any dead wood can be removed in late winter or early spring. On some of the large double-flowered varieties it may be necessary to support heavy blooms.
Propagation Species can be grown from seed. Named varieties and hybrids will not come true from seed. Layering in mid-spring is possible; two years are usually required for rooting to take place.
Pests and diseases There are fungus and viral diseases that can attack peonies. Also, swift moth caterpillars can eat the leaves.

ABOVE **Russian sage (*Perovskia* 'Blue Haze'), useful for its late flowers**

49. PEROVSKIA

Common name Russian sage
Family Lamiaceae

There are several species in this genus, but only one is in general cultivation, useful for its grey-green foliage and late-flowering habit.

Popular species and varieties

Perovskia atriplicifolia grows to 1m (3ft) in height and produces sprays of lavender-blue flowers 30cm (12in) long. It is best in a border: the previous year's stems are cut back to a few inches above the soil in late winter, consequently it is not particularly attractive until well into summer.

These plants are valuable for their flowering which commences in mid-summer and usually continues until early autumn. There are a small number of named varieties, the most popular being 'Blue Spire' (AGM).

Another excellent form is 'Blue Haze'. Both of these perovskias have attractive violet-blue flowers and small, grey, daintily cut foliage. If the leaves are crushed they give off an aroma similar to sage.

Cultivation

Soil type Most humus-rich, well-drained soils are suitable for perovskias.
Planting Choose a sunny spot. Plant in late autumn or spring, whenever soil conditions allow.
Maintenance Cut back in the spring to a few inches above ground level.
Propagation Semi-ripe cuttings with a heel can be taken in the summer.
Pests and diseases Normally, no problems are experienced with these shrubs.

GARDENING WITH **SHRUBS**

PLANT DIRECTORY

50. PHILADELPHUS

Common name Mock orange
Family Hydrangeaceae

These very desirable summer-flowering shrubs are noted for their fragrance, reminiscent of orange blossom, hence their common name.

The *Philadelphus* genus contains free-flowering shrubs, and they very usefully fill a gap between the spring and summer displays. In addition they are easy to grow: poor soils, exposed positions, salt-laden atmosphere – they take it all in their stride.

Popular species and varieties

Among the most popular is 'Belle Etoile' (AGM), which grows to 3m (10ft) and has masses of single white, purple-throated flowers that are particularly fragrant. 'Virginal' (AGM) is unquestionably one of the most popular of the hybrids. The flowers are white, double, and cup shaped, and are carried in pendent clusters.

Among the species readily available is *Philadelphus coronarius*, which has creamy white single flowers in early summer. One to look for is *P. coronarius* 'Variegatus' (AGM), whose foliage has creamy white margins. With rich, golden foliage, 'Aureus' (AGM) is another good variety for creating contrast.

There are also members of this family with a dwarf habit. For example, 'Manteau d'Hermine' (AGM) grows to just 60cm (24in) in height, with fragrant cream-white double blooms.

Cultivation

Soil type Most ordinary garden soils are suitable provided they are well drained.
Planting This can be done in the autumn or spring, in a sunny or lightly shaded spot.
Pruning Attention is required immediately after flowering when some of the old wood should be cut out. Take care not to damage new growth which will carry flowers the following year.
Propagation Take semi-ripe cuttings around 10cm (4in) long in the summer, or hardwood cuttings in late autumn.
Pests and diseases Aphids can be a problem on new growth: spray as soon as seen with an insecticide.

LEFT *Philadelphus* 'Belle Etoile': an old favourite with fragrant pure white flowers

GARDENING WITH **SHRUBS**

51. PHOTINIA

Common name none
Family Rosaceae

Many members of this family grow too large for the average garden. It is the named varieties of the evergreen *Photinia* x *fraseri* that have the most appeal, mainly for the colour of their new growth.

Popular species and varieties

There are three worth considering. 'Birmingham' is an old favourite introduced in the early 1940s. Its foliage is a dark coppery red especially in spring. 'Robusta' (AGM) is, as its name indicates, stronger growing, and has bright red leaves.

Without doubt the best is 'Red Robin' (AGM). Raised in New Zealand, it is most attractive with bright scarlet-bronze new growth that in time mellows to a reddish bronze. These shrubs will grow to 3m (10ft) or more in height.

Cultivation

Soil type Well-drained, moist and humus-rich.
Planting The evergreen photinias are happy in a sunny or lightly shaded spot, but they will not do well in exposed windy sites.
Maintenance Regular pruning is not necessary; any old straggly growth can be cut back in the spring.
Propagation Semi-ripe cuttings can be taken in early summer.
Pests and diseases Generally trouble free.

LEFT The young foliage of *Photinia* x *fraseri* 'Birmingham' is copper-red

52. PIERIS

Common name Andromeda
Family Ericaceae

These handsome slow-growing evergreen shrubs with their graceful sprays of bell-shaped flowers, in many ways reminiscent of lily of the valley, have become very popular in recent years. Some varieties, particularly 'Forest Flame' (AGM), are noted for their brilliant red new growths in spring. One thing that must never be forgotten is that they are lime-haters, so acid soil conditions are essential.

Popular species and varieties

Today there are a considerable number of species and varieties from which to choose. Among those with white flowers are *Pieris formosa*, 'Forest Flame' (AGM), 'Firecrest' (AGM), and 'Wakehurst' (AGM); all have vivid red new spring growth. Flowering takes place from late winter until mid-spring.

There are some with dusky rose-pink blooms, and these are equally as attractive. They include 'Blush' (AGM), the young growth in this case is coppery-red, and 'Flamingo' with dark red buds opening to deep pink.

Cultivation

Soil type Moist, lime-free soils are essential.
Planting This can be carried out in the autumn or spring. Choose a lightly shaded spot where they are sheltered from cold winds. The new growth and buds of *Pieris* are vulnerable to frost. Top-dress the soil around the base of the shrubs annually in spring, using well-rotted leaf mould or peat.
Pruning Pruning is not generally required – any straggly branches can be removed in late winter if required. The flowers should be snipped off as soon as they have faded.
Propagation Take cuttings of half-ripe shoots, approximately 10cm (4in) long, in mid-summer. Layering is also possible although it usually takes two years for a good root system to form.
Pests and diseases Normally no problems are experienced with these shrubs.

ABOVE *Pieris formosa* is grown for its bright red, young foliage

ABOVE Raised in New Zealand, *Pittosporum tenuifolium* 'Tom Thumb' is a dense, rounded, dwarf shrub

53. PITTOSPORUM

Common name none
Family Pittosporaceae

The *Pittosporum* genus is grown principally for its attractive and distinctive foliage. Many originate from the southern hemisphere and are of uncertain hardiness in the north. They cope well in salt-laden atmospheres. The flowers are small, and bell-shaped or tubular, and in many cases fragrant.

Popular species and varieties

The species best known is *Pittosporum tenuifolium*, a native of New Zealand, a slow-growing shrub with pale green, wavy leaves carried on black stems. In mild districts it can be used for hedging or screening.

There are a number of named varieties, among them 'Purpureum', with leaves that turn to rich bronze-purple. 'Gold Star' is a compact shrub; its foliage has a yellow-green blotch in the centre. 'Tom Thumb' (AGM) forms a dense, rounded shrub with distinctive reddish purple leaves. 'Warnham Gold' (AGM) is a real eye-catcher – the young growth is greenish yellow and, as it ages, it turns to a golden yellow. It looks particularly attractive during the winter months.

Cultivation

Soil type Well-drained, fertile soil.
Planting Choose a warm spot where they are not subjected to cold winds. Plant out in early to mid-spring.
Pruning Keep the shrub in good shape by removing any odd shoots in the spring. Any frost-damaged branches should also be removed at this time. If grown as a hedge, trim in late spring.
Propagation In early summer, take semi-ripe cuttings with a heel. Overwinter the cuttings in a frost-free frame or greenhouse.
Pests and diseases Problems are unlikely.

54. POTENTILLA

Common name Shrubby cinquefoil
Family Rosaceae

If any garden shrub could be described as 'indispensable' it is the *Potentilla*. It is generally easily grown, requiring little attention, happy in sun or light shade and, above all, flowering from late spring to early autumn.

Over the years, the naming of these plants has, to say the least, become somewhat confused so it is best to rely on variety name. Potentillas are available in several colours, with yellows and whites leading the field. However, those with pink or red flowers are equally attractive (these are best grown in a lightly shaded spot as their blooms tend to fade when subjected to the full glare of the sun).

One has only to look through a specialist shrub catalogue to appreciate just how many potentillas there are. Most are small or medium-sized.

Popular species and varieties

Among the many yellows are 'Elizabeth' (AGM) and 'Primrose Beauty' (AGM), both growing to about 1m (3ft) in height, with large canary-yellow blooms. 'Golden Spreader' is a good low-growing potentilla with masses of deep yellow flowers. 'Lemon and Lime' is free-flowering with light green-yellow blooms.

One of the best known white varieties is 'Abbotswood' (AGM), growing to 75cm (30in) in height. 'Manchin' is a good ground cover shrub, just 30cm (12in) high. One that created a considerable stir when introduced a few years ago was the vermillion 'Red Ace'. This is another low grower, reaching just 60cm (24in). Another excellent choice is 'Hopley's Orange' with blooms of, would you believe, orange. There are, as already mentioned, plenty more from which to choose.

Cultivation

Soil type Any well-drained soils – but ideally not too rich, as this would result in foliage at the expense of flowers.
Planting Sun or light shade, the latter is best for reds and oranges. They can be planted whenever conditions are suitable from early autumn to early spring.
Maintenance No general pruning is required, but keep the plants in shape by removing any weak or straggly growth in the spring.
Propagation Semi-ripe cuttings with a heel, taken in summer.
Pests and diseases Generally, no problems are encountered.

ABOVE *Potentilla* 'Lemon and Lime'

GARDENING WITH **SHRUBS**

55. PRUNUS

Common name Ornamental cherry

Family Rosaceae

Many *Prunus* are trees that make a fine springtime show, but there are also many valuable shrubby forms for the garden.

Popular species and varieties

One that seldom fails to attract attention is *Prunus tenella* 'Fire Hill' (AGM), a deciduous shrub growing to around 1.2m (4ft), and which covers its stems with rose-red blooms in late winter and early spring.

Originating in the USA, the deciduous *P.* x *cistena* (AGM) is often used for hedging and grows to around 2.4m (7ft) in height. In early spring white flowers and deep red foliage are produced. Widely known as the dwarf crimson cherry or the cherry plum, *Prunus cerasifera* can be used for taller hedging, although it will eventually grow into a small tree. It is deciduous and flowers in early spring. One of the most attractive is *P. cerasifera* 'Pissardii', with white flowers that are followed by deep purple leaves.

Cultivation

Soil type Most well-drained soils are suitable.
Planting Choose a sunny spot, and plant in the autumn or spring.
Maintenance No regular pruning is required, but damaged or unwanted shoots should be removed in late summer.
Propagation With *P. tenella*, take heel cuttings in late spring. Hardwood cuttings can be taken of *P. cerasifera* in late autumn; root them in a nursery bed.
Pests and diseases These shrubs can be affected by several fungal diseases.

LEFT *Prunus tenella* **'Fire Hill' flowers freely in early spring**

GARDENING WITH **SHRUBS**

PLANT DIRECTORY

56. PYRACANTHA

Common name Firethorn
Family Rosaceae

Pyracantha is usually grown as a shrub. It is not hard to see how it gained its common name: the plant has sharp spines and a fine display in the autumn and winter of red and orange berries. Whenever you have to handle this shrub, always wear strong gloves. It proves a good barrier around property to keep out intruders, and it can also be grown as a free-standing shrub (but be careful to position it carefully because of its spines).

Masses of white flowers are produced in spring. Attractive as these are, it is for the dense clusters of vivid berries that this shrub is grown.

Popular species and varieties
The majority of pyracanthas offered for sale are garden hybrids. 'Orange Glow' (AGM) forms a dense medium-sized shrub, and in the autumn it is covered with long-lasting bright orange-red berries. It is a vigorous plant that can grow up to 5m (15ft) if left unchecked.

One form that is very popular is 'Soleil d'Or', which has a spreading habit and produces rich deep yellow berries. An old favourite, and excellent for hedging, is 'Watereri' (AGM), which has compact, bushy growth, very dark green leaves, and freely produces bright red berries.

'Mohave' is one pyracantha that retains its berries throughout winter, as birds do not like them. This vigorous and wide-spreading shrub produces dense clusters of small red berries.

Cultivation
Soil type Any good garden soil.
Planting Autumn or spring, in sun or light shade.
Pruning Remove any unwanted or damaged branches in late winter or early spring. When grown on a wall cut back the long growths immediately after flowering.
Propagating Semi-ripe cuttings with a heel should be taken in early to mid-summer.
Pests and diseases As with other members of the rose family, this can be attacked by fireblight disease.

LEFT *Pyracantha coccinea* – masses of flowers, but watch out for the spines

GARDENING WITH **SHRUBS**

57. RHODODENDRON

Common name none
Family Ericaceae

There are numerous rhododendrons that are capable, when in flower and when grown well, of stopping you in your tracks. They are available in a wide range of sizes, from large tree-like specimens and larger shrubs, down to ground huggers that are suitable for the rock garden or front of a border. Many are grown for their rich vibrant colours, others are more subtle with pastel shades. Azaleas – one of the smaller-leaved forms of rhododendron – usually have the most brilliant coloured flowers.

It is a huge family, with a considerable number of species and legions of named varieties, the results of many years of hybridization. Some are evergreen and some deciduous. Some have individual leaves the size of paddle blades, whilst the smallest is around 1.5cm (¾in). Some rhododendrons flower in early winter and are best grown in mild districts in sheltered spots. The majority bloom in the spring.

Rhododendrons are lime-haters and require acid soil conditions, so are not suitable for some districts. Where the soil itself is a problem, some of the more compact varieties can be grown in large containers in ericaceous compost, but ensure they do not become dry in hot weather.

Popular species and varieties

The large-flowered hybrid rhododendrons are among the most popular of all shrubs, and are readily found at garden centres. This in no way detracts from the charm of the species themselves. When it comes to choice it is difficult to know where to start. Among those with red blooms are 'Baden Baden', a good dwarf variety, and 'Britannia' (AGM), an old favourite. One very popular for smaller gardens is the bright orange-red 'Dopey' (AGM).

Always eye-catching are the yellows. Among the best are 'Hotei' (AGM), medium sized with masses of deep yellow bell-shaped blooms, and 'Queen Elizabeth II' (AGM), a free-flowering medium variety with greenish-yellow, wide, funnel-shaped blooms.

For white flowers there is 'Helene Schiffner' (AGM), an old stager but still among the best. The buds are mauve to start with, opening to reveal pure white flowers. One white was introduced as long ago as 1867: 'Sappho' (AGM). Here again the buds are mauve, but the pure white flowers have a rich purple blotch.

'Percy Wiseman' (AGM) is a compact plant with white flushed pink blooms; 'Purple Splendour' (AGM) is, as its name indicates, a rich deep purple, and 'Morgenrot' (AGM) is a lovely rose red.

Deciduous hybrid azaleas

Well known for their free-flowering habit and range of colours, the deciduous azaleas range in height from 1.5–2.5m (5–9ft). These also require acid soil conditions and preferably a sheltered spot in light shade. Among those to look for are the flame-orange 'Gibralter' (AGM), and 'Glowing Embers', best described as a reddish orange. 'Satan' (AGM) is a lovely geranium-red, and 'Persil' (AGM) has masses of white blooms with an orange-yellow flare.

Evergreen hybrid group

These are widely referred to as Japanese azaleas. They are excellent, low-growing shrubs ranging from 0.6–1.2m (2–4ft) in height, and are grown for their masses of late spring and early summer flowers. They often completely cover themselves with blooms so that the foliage is hidden. Two great favourites are the very dwarf 'Hatsugiri' (AGM), a striking magenta purple, and

LEFT *Rhododendron* 'Morgenrot' (syn. 'Morning Red') – compact and free-flowering the taller 'Hinomayo' (AGM), a lovely clear pink. Equally as attractive are the rose-red 'Mother's Day' (AGM), and the white 'Palestrina' (AGM). One you can hardly fail to miss for its sizeable bright red blooms is 'Vuyk's Scarlet' (AGM). These azaleas provide a magnificent show when grouped together; sometimes colour clashes are thought to be desirable, but I try to avoid them.

Cultivation

Soil type Acid soil is essential; it should be moist but not waterlogged. The ideal conditions are sandy loam, which does not dry out. Adding peat or leaf mould will help to retain moisture on lighter soils.

Planting Most rhododendrons, especially those with larger leaves, are best grown in a lightly shaded spot where they are not subjected to cold winds. Many will grow happily in full sun provided sufficient moisture is available at all times. Any that flower before the late spring should be positioned where the flowers are not in sunlight in the early morning, as after a frost these can be damaged. Planting can be carried out in the autumn or spring. The rootball should be set just below soil level and topped with a mulch of peat or leaf mould. Ensure the plants are well watered, and keep the soil moist in dry weather.

Pruning Regular pruning is not required, but any straggly growth can be removed in the spring. Dead-heading, where possible, is an advantage but take care not to damage growth buds at the base of the flower.

Propagation Increasing rhododendrons takes quite a time. This is best done by layering or, in some cases, cuttings from those with small leaves. Unless you are skilled in the art of propagating rhododendrons, and have plenty of room and time, it is probably best to consider buying any new plants you require.

Pests and diseases One problem that can be encountered in unsuitable soils is yellowing of the leaves, which is known as chlorosis. Watering with a sequestered iron compound will help, but only temporarily if lime is present. There are a number of fungal diseases that can attack rhododendrons.

RIGHT *Rhododendron 'Crest'*
– an acid soil is essential

PLANT DIRECTORY

GARDENING WITH **SHRUBS**

ABOVE **The stag's horn sumach (*Rhus typhina*)**

58. RHUS

Common name Sumach
Family Ancardiaceae

One of the best known members of this family, grown principally for the foliage and autumn colour is the stag's horn sumach (*Rhus typhina*) (AGM). A native of North America, it has been in cultivation since the 1600s. The sap of the sumach can cause skin irritation, so precautions should be taken when handling.

Popular species and varieties

Rhus typhina (AGM) forms a large, spreading shrub with suckering stems. In the autumn the leaves take on a mixture of rich orange, yellow and red. When they fall they leave behind crimson, hair-covered fruits that last well into winter, turning dark brown as they age.

One of the best forms is *R. typhina* 'Dissecta' (AGM), the leaves of which are dissected providing a fern-like effect. It also takes on rich autumn colours and has crimson seed heads. Another rhus that has been in cultivation for centuries is the smooth sumach (*Rhus glabra*). It is a medium-sized shrub with shiny, deeply toothed leaves that turn to an intense orange and red in the autumn. The female plants, in this case, have dramatic hair-covered, scarlet, plume-like flower heads.

Cultivation

Soil type Most well-drained soils are suitable.
Planting This can be done between early autumn and late winter whenever soil conditions allow. Choose a sunny spot.
Pruning No pruning is required. *R. glabra* and *R. typhina* can be cut down to ground level in mid to late winter, which will encourage additional shoots and an abundance of foliage.
Propagation Cuttings of half-ripe shoots around 10cm (4in) long, taken with a heel, in mid to late summer. Suckers can be removed in early autumn and planted elsewhere. Alternatively, shoots can be layered in the spring; these will usually be ready in two years.
Pests and diseases Rhus can suffer from die-back caused by unsuitable soil or weather conditions, otherwise this genus is generally trouble free.

59. RIBES

Common name
Ornamental currant

Family Grossulariaceae

Following hard on the heels of the forsythia is the widely grown flowering currant (*Ribes sanguineum*). A deciduous species with pink flowers in clusters, it is native to North America and was introduced to European gardens in the early 19th century.

Popular species and varieties

While the species itself will provide a colourful show, it is the numerous named varieties that are the most popular. Among them are 'Pulborough Scarlet' (AGM), a widely available shrub, and 'King Edward VII', slow-growing and noted for its intense red flowers. It is worth searching for 'Elk River Red' and 'White Icicle', both names of which clearly describe the flower colours. Do not overlook 'Brocklebankii' (AGM), which grows to 1m (3ft) and has pink flowers with golden foliage. It is best in a lightly shaded spot, as it tends to burn in full sun. Its flowers are usually followed by black berries.

One evergreen member of this family, which created much interest when it was introduced from China in 1912 by Ernest Wilson, is *Ribes laurifolium*. It has large leathery leaves. The clusters of greenish-white flowers appear in mid-winter, and are followed by red berries which slowly turn black if male and female forms are grown together. This is an ideal shrub for a sizeable rock garden, where it adds interest at a bleak time of the year.

Cultivation

Soil type Most well-drained garden soils are suitable.
Planting All forms of *Ribes* are happy in sunny or lightly shaded spots. Planting can be carried out whenever conditions are suitable, between early autumn and early spring. Keep plants well watered in dry spells until they are fully established.
Pruning Cut back flowered shoots in early summer and remove old wood. Top-dress the ground around the base of the plants with well-rotted manure or garden compost, in early spring.
Propagation Cuttings, either semi-ripe taken in late spring or early summer, or hardwood taken during mid-autumn. Propagate *R. laurifolium* with 7cm (3in) cuttings in September.
Pests and diseases Aphids can be a nuisance on new and young growth, but these are easily dealt with by using a suitable insecticide.

ABOVE *Ribes laurifolium* – a low-growing, evergreen species flowering in late winter

ABOVE *Rosa* 'Madame Isaac Pereire' – large, fragrant, cup-shaped blooms

60. ROSA

Common name Rose
Family Rosaceae

There must be few gardens where you cannot find at least one example of the huge rose family. There are climbers, ramblers, English roses, free-flowering floribundas, the immensely popular hybrid teas, wild roses and their hybrids, not forgetting the miniature and 'patio' roses, popular for today's trend towards smaller gardens.

Roses have been in cultivation since very early times, principally for medicinal uses and sometimes for religious ceremonial purposes. Using roses purely for their decorative attributes in gardens is a much more recent occurrence.

Glance through a catalogue of a specialist rose grower and you will find hundreds of varieties, many of which have a long history and are still as popular as ever. Among these is the rose known variously as the apothecary's rose, or the red rose of Lancaster (*Rosa gallica* var. *officinalis*) (AGM). It is a fragrant example of great antiquity. A variation of this is *R. gallica* 'Versicolor', with the same wonderful fragrance; it dates back to even before the 16th century.

Popular species and varieties

For many it is the elegant hybrid tea roses, or bush roses as they are also known, that have the greatest attraction. They have exquisitely formed pointed buds that open to reveal their sumptuous blooms. The modern hybrid teas are much stronger and healthier

ABOVE **The hybrid tea 'Just Joey' – makes a good flower for cutting**

than the early varieties that date back to the 1860s. Selective breeding over the years has improved the plants and the flowers, to end up with the superb examples we have today.

The hybrid tea is a rose difficult to beat – some are fragrant in varying degrees, others have no fragrance at all. They are available in a range of bold and pastel shades, among these crimson, scarlet and vermillion, to the rich golds and yellows and the more delicate apricots, oranges and so on. From the hundreds of varieties available, there are three I would like to recommend: 'Just Joey' (AGM) carries elegant buds of coppery orange veined with red, 'Velvet Fragrance', deep crimson, and 'Peace' (AGM), a great favourite, with light yellow blooms flushed with pink.

Floribunda roses

If you wish to create a mass of colour, the floribundas should be considered. These free-flowering shrubs have a long season. They are not noted for their fragrance but they are hardy, robust, more disease-resistant and easy to grow. One of the best is still the bright vermillion-red 'Trumpeter' (AGM), a compact bush introduced in 1977.

English roses

This is a fairly new group of roses that came to prominence in the 1970s, the result of crosses between old roses, hybrid teas and floribundas. The charm and fragrance of the former has been combined with the repeat flowering and colour range found within the latter two. English roses have shrubby growth, are free-flowering, and are usually highly fragrant, which makes them immensely popular.

Every year there are new introductions, and among those to look for are 'Corvedale' with cup-shaped pink blooms, 'Gertrude Jekyll' (AGM), soft pink, and 'Tess of the D'Urbervilles', bright crimson. There are many more in bright and pastel shades, also spray-flowered, and varieties that can be trained as climbers.

Old roses

These flower in the summer, when they give a truly splendid display, and there are several distinct groups.
- The 'Gallicas' are the oldest garden roses, with elegant, beautifully formed blooms. A typical example is 'Cardinal De Richelieu' (AGM), very dark purple.
- The 'Albas', which go back to the middle ages,

include 'Alba Semiplena' (AGM), a very fragrant single with milk-white flowers.

● The 'Damasks' are also very old, said to have been introduced from the Middle East by the Crusaders. They are wonderfully fragrant, and one of the best is 'Marie-Louise', a full-petalled intense pink.

The remaining groups are the 'Centifolias' (Provence roses), and the 'Mosses', noted for their fragrant oil. Some of the best rose displays are provided by the climbing and rambling species and varieties. These are best grown and trained on walls, pillars, arches and pergolas – even 'catenaries' or hanging ropes make attractive structures for roses.

Climbers are different to ramblers, in that they have larger flowers, including climbing versions of bush varieties such as 'Ena Harkness' and 'Gertrude Jekyll'. The singles include 'Mermaid', a fragrant sulphur yellow, and 'Golden Showers' (AGM), well known for its large semi-double, golden-yellow blooms produced over a long period.

The ramblers bloom with great freedom and produce masses of flowers, once a year in the majority of cases. 'Crimson Shower' (AGM) is a good example and one noted for its long season, usually lasting from mid-summer through to early autumn. Its trusses of flowers are bright crimson, set off well by dark foliage.

Patio roses

Recent years have seen garden patios become a main feature of many gardens. As a result, more roses listed as suitable for patios have become available. These are low growing, are ideal for the smaller garden, and are offered in a range of colours.

One of the most popular is 'Hakuun' with masses of small buff-orange blooms on bushy plants 45cm (18in) high. 'Flower Power' is another extremely free-flowering variety with salmon-pink flowers and a spicy fragrance. It has a low, compact habit and does not exceed 30cm (12in). Growing to twice the height, but well worth considering, is 'Miss Edith Cavell', an old stager with scarlet-crimson flowers held in small trusses.

One should not overlook the miniature roses that grow to 30–45cm (12–18in), ideal for very small gardens, window boxes and containers. These have a profusion of tiny miniature blooms. One of the best is 'Stars'n'Stripes', with red and white striped blooms held on sturdy 30cm (12in) high stems.

Cultivation

Soil type Most soils are suitable, with the exception of pure sand, chalk and very heavy 'blue' clay. Roses will not tolerate waterlogged conditions.

Planting Choose an open, sunny position where they are not subjected to cold winds. Before planting, incorporate plenty of well-rotted manure or compost. Avoid fresh animal manure, which is harmful to the roots. Ideally, prepare the bed in late summer or early autumn for planting to take place three or four weeks afterwards. Roses can be planted any time up to early spring, as long as soil conditions are suitable. Dig a large hole, incorporate a handful of bonemeal, spread the roots into position so that they are not cramped or bent, and firm the soil well afterwards. Standard roses should be staked; climbers and ramblers tied to supports.

Pruning New roses planted in the autumn or winter should be pruned early in the spring. The idea is to produce a framework of strong shoots, at the same time giving the plant a chance to establish quickly. Pruning is generally severe: hybrid teas should be cut back to two or three buds from the base, floribundas four or five. With climbers and ramblers, retain about 45cm (18in) of the strongest growth. Any weak shoots can be cut back to 7–10cm (3–4in) from the base of the plant. This initial pruning should not be overlooked, as it will result in the production of a strong framework of growth from low on the plant.

Established roses are pruned in late winter. Species and shrub roses require little more than the removal of any straggly stems. Hybrid tea roses, for garden decoration, should have the strongest shoots cut back to four to six buds of the base of the previous year's growth. Take out any weaker stems to between two and four buds. Avoid cutting into any wood that is more than one year old. Retain a good shape, prune to an outward-facing bud where possible, and remove any congested or crossing stems. The floribundas should be reduced to five to seven buds from the base, and any weak shoots cut back hard.

With climbing roses, a framework of branches is established and trained into position in the early years. Cut back short, lateral shoots to two or three buds in the spring. Any vigorous young growth coming up from the base should be tied into the framework, without pruning. In time this will be used to replace any old branches that require removal.

ABOVE *Rosa rugosa* 'Alba'

A different treatment is required for ramblers as these flower on previous years' growth, which is produced annually from ground level. As a result, when flowering has finished cut down old stems to ground level. Tie in new shoots and, if desired, some of the old shoots can be left for a second year. Pruning should be by cutting back the laterals to two or three buds from their base.

Propagation Hardwood cuttings from shrub roses, ramblers and some others should be taken in late autumn, rooting them in an outdoor nursery bed. Taking cuttings of hybrid teas is not recommended as the resultant plants are likely to lack vigour. Miniature roses can be increased by taking 22cm (9in) cuttings with a heel from non-flowering shoots in late summer. The method most widely used by professional gardeners to increase many roses is by budding, but this is usually beyond the scope of most amateurs.

Pests and diseases There are a number of pests that attack roses (aphids, caterpillars, leafhoppers, sawflies, froghoppers and so on), and these can be dealt with by using an appropriate insecticide. The most common disease to affect roses is black spot, which can be treated with a suitable fungicide. Some can also suffer from mildew, requiring similar treatment.

ABOVE *Rosmarinus officinalis* 'Severn Sea'

61. ROSMARINUS

Common name Rosemary
Family Lamiaceae

These are evergreen shrubs, often classed as 'herbs'. Although there are other species available, it is *Rosmarinus officinalis*, a native of Mediterranean regions, that is the one usually seen in our gardens. There are also numerous named varieties.

Popular species and varieties

Rosmarinus officinalis grows to around 1.5m (5ft) and has narrow grey-green leaves. In late spring and early summer, clusters of blue flowers appear along the branches of the previous years' growth. Among the numerous forms is 'Benenden Blue', which was originally found in Corsica. This is a smaller form than the straight species, with bright blue flowers. It should be given a sheltered spot. One that is hardy in all but the most severe winters is 'Miss Jessup's Upright' (AGM). Previously known as 'Fastigiatus', it can still occasionally be referred to by this name. Widely available, it has typical blue flowers.

Another worth considering is 'Sissinghurst Blue' (AGM), a good blue with a free-flowering habit.

Plants that can be used as ground cover, or for hanging over a wall, are particularly useful in the garden, and the accommodating *Rosmarinus* 'Prostratus Group' (AGM), with large, dense mats of pale blue, will do both of these.

Cultivation

Soil type Rosemary will grow in most fertile, well-drained soils.
Planting Choose a sunny spot, ideally where it is not subjected to cold winds. Plant in the spring.
Pruning Pruning consists of cutting out any dead wood in early spring. After flowering, shorten any long straggly shoots. Any old bushes can be improved by cutting back shoots to half their length, in early spring.
Propagation This herby shrub is easily increased by semi-ripe cuttings taken during early to mid-summer, or mature shoots in late summer.
Pests and diseases No problems are normally encountered with these shrubs.

PLANT DIRECTORY

ABOVE *Rubus biflorus* – its silver stems brighten up the winter garden

62. RUBUS

Common name **Ornamental bramble**
Family **Rosaceae**

Some of our well-known soft fruits (raspberries, blackberries and the modern hybrid berries) are members of the *Rubus* genus, but these are beyond the scope of this book. There are, however, several ornamental shrubs valued for their attractive and colourful winter stems.

Popular species and varieties

The most popular member of this genus is *Rubus cockburnianus* (AGM), introduced from China by the plant hunter Ernest Wilson in 1907. It is a deciduous shrub grown for its winter stems which are purple overlaid with a heavy, vivid white bloom.
R. cockburnianus 'Goldenvale' (AGM) has the added advantage of having golden-yellow foliage. Among the flowering types is the deciduous hybrid 'Benenden' (AGM) which has thornless shoots stretching to 3m (10ft) or more. In mid-spring these have 5cm (2in) wide blooms of pure white, with golden-yellow stamens along their length.

Cultivation

Soil type All forms of *Rubus* are happy in good well-drained soil.
Planting This can be done between early autumn and late winter, whenever conditions are suitable. Choose a sunny or lightly shaded spot.
Pruning Pruning consists of cutting back in the autumn some of the older stems to ground level. Also, remove any damaged or dead branches at this time.
Propagation Take semi-ripe cuttings of around 7–10cm (3–4in) in the summer.
Pests and diseases Normally no problems are experienced with these cane shrubs.

GARDENING WITH **SHRUBS**

63. SALIX

Common name Willow
Family Salicaceae

This large genus includes many that are large trees. But there are also plenty of good garden shrubs, with some low-growing and ground hugging examples. Willows are grown principally for their impressive displays of catkins in the late winter and spring.

Popular species and varieties

One form that has a low-growing habit is *Salix lanata* (AGM), which does not grow more than 1m (36in) in height, but can easily exceed this figure in spread. It has soft, silvery foliage and woolly, yellow-grey catkins that can be up to 10cm (4in) long. The variety 'Stuarti' can have even longer catkins. *Salix hastata* 'Wehrhahnii' (AGM) also grows to around the same height. It was discovered in Switzerland in the early 1930s and has wonderful silvery grey catkins. Another, also from the Alps, is *S. helvetica* (AGM), a neat bushy shrub that grows to around 60cm (24in) and has a profusion of silver-grey catkins.

One very desirable salix which was discovered in the 1870s growing on a Scottish mountainside, is *S. x boydii* (AGM), undoubtedly the slowest growing – even after many years it may still be just 75cm (30in) in height. It forms a small gnarled shrub with downy grey-green leaves. Only very occasionally will it produce catkins. It is a good subject for the rock garden.

In the late 1970s, *S. integra* 'Hakuru Nishiki' was introduced; it is very different to those already mentioned. Raised in Japan, it has white blotched foliage held on polished stems. It is very effective in a waterside planting, but can burn in very strong sunlight – a lightly shaded spot is best.

Cultivation

Soil type Most moisture-retentive soils are suitable.
Planting Willows are happy in sun or light shade. Planting can be done whenever conditions are suitable, between early autumn and late winter.
Pruning General pruning is not required, but any damaged or unwanted branches can be removed in late winter.
Propagation Hardwood cuttings around 22cm (9in) long may be taken from early autumn; root them in a nursery bed.
Pests and diseases Caterpillars, aphids and scale insects can be a problem: treat with suitable insecticide as soon as seen.

LEFT The woolly willow (*Salix lanata*) is ideal for the larger rock garden

GARDENING WITH SHRUBS

ABOVE *Santolina pinnata* – a small, aromatic shrub native to Italy

64. SANTOLINA

Common name Cotton lavender
Family Asteraceae

These low-growing shrubs originating from Mediterranean regions are grown for their attractive silvery foliage and small button-like flowers.

Popular species and varieties

One species with bright lemon-yellow summer flowers over silver-white feathery foliage is *Santolina pinnata* subsp. *neapolitana* (AGM). The form that is most widely seen in gardens is *S. chamaecyparissus* (AGM), which grows to round 60cm (24in) and has silvery foliage and bright yellow blooms, although flowering can sometimes be a little disappointing. It has been grown in our gardens since the 16th century.

Santolina rosmarinifolia is a very dwarf species and best grown on the rock garden. The foliage, in this case, is bright green, highlighting the equally bright lemon-yellow flowers that appear in early summer.

Cultivation

Soil type Most well-drained soils – *Santolina* will not tolerate cold, waterlogged conditions.
Planting These are sun-lovers; plant them in the autumn or spring. The latter has the advantage in that plants will establish quicker as soil temperatures rise.
Pruning Generally, all that is required is to trim the plants after flowering. Every two or three years cut them back hard to encourage new growth from the base, and to keep the plant tidy.
Propagation Semi-ripe cuttings around 5–7cm (2–3in) long should be taken in summer.
Pests and diseases Generally trouble free.

ABOVE *Senecio greyi* (syn. *Brachyglottis* 'Sunshine') is grown more for its silvery foliage than its flowers

65. SENECIO

Common name none
Family Asteraceae

Shrubs with silvery foliage are particularly useful for adding variety to the border, and it is for this reason and for its bright yellow daisy-like flowers that *Senecio* 'Sunshine' (AGM) is grown. This very popular and widely seen shrub is now more correctly listed under *Brachyglottis*, but it is still best known and most widely sold as senecio, so for this reason its former name is used here.

Popular species and varieties

'Sunshine' (AGM) is one of a group of hybrids raised in New Zealand. It has featured in our gardens for many years, and has been incorrectly known as S. *greyi* or S. *laxiflorus*. It is a rather lax, sprawling shrub around 1m (36in) in height. The foliage is silver-grey and stands up well to maritime conditions. In early summer loose heads of rather coarse, yellow daisy flowers appear.

Cultivation

Soil type Provided it is well-drained, any soil is suitable.
Planting Choose a sunny, sheltered spot. Plant in autumn or spring. This shrub is reasonably hardy but may not survive severe winters.
Pruning Maintain a neat shape by removing any dead or straggly shoots – do this at any time of year, apart from when it is in full bloom. To prolong the flowering period, remove flowers as they fade.
Propagation Take semi-ripe cuttings from non-flowering shoots in the summer.
Pests and diseases Generally trouble free.

ABOVE *Spiraea japonica* 'Goldflame'

66. SPIRAEA

Common name none
Family Rosaceae

These popular, quick-growing deciduous shrubs fall into two groups – the spring and the summer. They are particularly noted for their free-flowering habit.

Popular species and varieties

The best known form for spring flowering is the bridal wreath (*Spiraea* 'Arguta'). The slender arching branches are completely covered with clusters of pure white flowers in mid-spring, and the shrub will grow to around 2m (6ft). It is no stranger to our gardens having been grown for well over a hundred years. Also flowering in spring, and noted for its plentiful blooms, is *Spiraea* 'Grefsheim' (AGM).

The summer-flowering group is dominated by varieties of *S. japonica*. Probably the best known is 'Anthony Waterer' (AGM), which grows to 1m (3ft). The foliage is tinged with pink and cream, and it carries pink flowers for several weeks from early summer. 'Goldflame' (AGM), with rose-red flowers, is another good choice. The leaves, when young, are a reddish-orange, changing to gold and eventually green. 'Fire Light' is worth searching for – its young, bright orange-red foliage changes to orange-yellow and eventually pale green, before taking on a fiery red in the autumn. Finally, the dwarf 'Gold Mound' (AGM) grows to just 30cm (12in), with small heads of pink flowers from mid-summer.

Cultivation

Soil type Most fertile, well-drained soils are suitable.
Planting *Spiraea* is happy in full sun or lightly shaded positions. Plant whenever soil conditions are suitable from early autumn to late winter.
Pruning Those that flower in the spring only require old and weak growth to be cut out after flowering has finished. The summer-blooming group should be cut back in early spring to within 7–10cm (3–4in) of the ground.
Propagation Take semi-ripe cuttings in summer, or hardwood cuttings with a heel in autumn.
Pests and diseases One pest that can strip foliage is the larvae of sawflies. These can be controlled by using a contact insecticide as soon as they are seen.

ABOVE Lilac (*Syringa vulgaris*) was a great favourite in Victorian times

67. SYRINGA

Common name Lilac
Family Oleaceae

Syringa are large vigorous, suckering shrubs with fragrant flowers in late spring and early summer. They were great favourites in Victorian times, and after a period of decline they are now enjoying a well-deserved revival. The majority of lilacs grown today are cultivars originating from one species, the common lilac (*Syringa vulgaris*).

Popular species and varieties

There are single- and double-flowered lilacs available, all of which are sweetly scented. Several popular varieties today date back to the Victorian period, including 'Souvenir de Louis Spaeth', or now more correctly 'Andenken an Ludwig Spath' (AGM), which made its debut in 1883. Widely available, it is grown for its splendid wine-red blooms in long slender panicles. Others to look for are the deep reddish-purple 'Massena' and pure white 'Maud Notcutt'.

Those with double flowers are equally good, including 'President Grevy', lilac-blue, and 'Madame Lemoine' (AGM), an old favourite introduced in 1890 and without doubt one of the best whites. These lilacs all need space and are perhaps too large for most of today's generally smaller gardens.

Syringa microphylla grows to around 2m (6ft), and is a native of China. Look for the free-flowering form 'Superba' (AGM), with fragrant rose-pink flowers in abundance from mid to late spring.

Cultivation

Soil type Most garden soils, especially alkaline.
Planting This can be done in autumn, in either a sunny or lightly shaded spot. Lilacs usually take one or two seasons to settle down.
Pruning They can become a tangled mass of shoots, so cut out thin or unproductive branches and suckers, immediately after flowering. Remove dead flower heads.
Propagation The usual commercial method of increasing lilacs is by grafting. However, semi-ripe cuttings with a heel can be taken in the summer and rooted in a cold frame.
Pests and diseases There are several fungal diseases that can attack lilacs, although most are unlikely to encounter problems.

GARDENING WITH **SHRUBS**

68. VIBURNUM

Common name none
Family Caprifoliaceae

There are around 150 species of these generally easy-to-grow deciduous and evergreen shrubs, many noted for their wonderful fragrance. Some flower during the winter months on naked stems, whilst others bloom in the spring and summer. Some take on rich autumnal colours.

Popular species and varieties

Among the best known members of the family is *Viburnum* x *bodnantense*, a medium-sized shrub with a free-flowering habit. Its clusters of sweetly scented pink flowers on naked stems appear from mid-autumn, sometimes even earlier, and carry on throughout the winter. There are three forms (all AGM holders): 'Charles Lamont', rich pink; 'Dawn', rose pink gradually darkening as they age, and 'Deben', pink buds opening to white.

An excellent spring flowerer is *V.* x *burkwoodii*, an evergreen with dark foliage, green and shiny on the upper surface, brownish-grey and felted on the underside. The flower heads are pink in bud opening to white; unfortunately they do not last when cut. There are a number of named forms including 'Anne Russell' (AGM), grown for its fragrance and compact habit.

One species that flowers in the spring and early summer is *V. carlesii*. A native of Japan, when introduced in 1906 it soon became popular. There are a number of name varieties, perhaps the best being 'Aurora' (AGM) with coppery-tinted young foliage; its rose-red flower buds open to pale pink.

Viburnum davidii (AGM) is a low-growing evergreen shrub with large, oval, glossy dark green leaves. The flowers are small, in terminal clusters and appear in early summer. They are followed by long-lasting bright blue berries on reddish stalks. To ensure a good show it is necessary to have at least one male plant growing in close proximity.

With so many splendid plants available only a few can be mentioned. One should not overlook *V. tinus* with its evergreen oval leaves. This is a great favourite, widely planted and an excellent winter shrub. It has been in cultivation since it was introduced in the late 16th century from Mediterranean regions. The clusters of flat pink-budded flowers open to white and appear from late autumn. It is happy in sun or light shade and will tolerate maritime conditions.

Cultivation

Soil type Humus-rich, moist but well-drained soil.
Planting In autumn or spring, best in sun but will tolerate light shade. The winter-flowering varieties should be placed where they are not subjected to cold winds. Principally grown for their flowers, viburnums are best planted in groups of three or more.
Pruning Pruning is not generally required, except for cutting back damaged or straggly stems. Tackle the deciduous viburnums after flowering, and the evergreen forms in mid-spring.
Propagation Semi-ripe cuttings with a heel may be taken in late spring or early summer. Long shoots can be layered in late summer and detached a year later.
Pests and diseases Aphids can become a problem – as soon as they are noticed, spray them with a suitable insecticide.

LEFT *Viburnum carlesii* – a medium-sized shrub with fragrant flowers

GARDENING WITH **SHRUBS**

ABOVE *Weigela florida* 'Variegata' – one of the best variegated shrubs

69. **WEIGELA**

Common name none
Family Caprifoliaceae

These free-flowering, medium-sized shrubs are ideal for smaller gardens, as they grow to around 2m (6ft). In late spring and early summer they can be relied upon to provide a colourful display.

Popular species and varieties

The most popular is *Weigela florida*, first introduced from the Far East in 1845. Look for 'Variegata' (AGM), which has tubular rose-pink flowers edged with cream, over attractive mid-green foliage. It is regarded generally as being one of the best variegated shrubs for the garden.

Among the many hybrids that are widely available is the aptly named ruby-red 'Bristol Ruby'. Also there is 'Abel Carriere' (AGM), another old favourite that has been around for over 100 years. It is among the first to flower, producing a profusion of rose-pink blooms in mid-spring. Do not overlook 'Newport Red', a splendid shrub that produces a fine show of light red blossoms. Finally, 'Mont Blanc' lives up well to its name, and is not a newcomer by any means.

Cultivation

Soil type Any reasonable fertile soil, including alkaline.
Planting This can be carried out in autumn or spring, whenever ground conditions are suitable. Select a sunny spot or one that is lightly shaded.
Pruning As soon as the flowers have faded, cut back flowering shoots to within a short distance of old wood.
Propagation Hardwood cuttings with a heel may be taken in late autumn.
Pests and diseases Normally without problems.

PLANT DIRECTORY

70. YUCCA

Common name none
Family Agavaceae

These architectural, evergreen shrubs with rosettes of sharply pointed narrow leaves, and tall spikes made up of masses of bell-shaped blooms, give an exotic look to the border.

Popular species and varieties

Adam's needle (*Yucca filamentosa*) (AGM) is a native of the SE United States. Its common name is due to its stiff, narrow, shiny leaves. Flowering usually commences when the plant is two or three years old. In early and mid-summer it produces a tall spike with numerous cream-white flowers. Look for the form 'Variegata' (AGM), with attractive leaves edged with a broad yellow and cream margin.

One yucca that does not flower until it is at least five years old is *Yucca gloriosa* (AGM), a larger plant that forms dense rosettes of deep green leaves. The creamy white flower spike appears in late summer, and is usually up to 2m (6ft) in height.

Cultivation

Soil type Good, well-drained, humus-rich soils are required.
Planting Either early autumn or mid-spring in a sunny spot. One point to remember is that yuccas have stiff, sharp, pointed leaves, so avoid spots near paths or children's play areas.
Pruning No pruning is required, except to cut off any dead leaves.
Propagation Rooted offsets can often be found at the base of the plant. Carefully remove these and grow them on for two or three years in a pot, when they will be large enough to plant out.
Pests and diseases Generally trouble free.

RIGHT The tropical-looking *Yucca gloriosa*

CHAPTER EIGHT

HANDY
GUIDES

Shrubs for specific places

LEFT *Potentilla* 'Golden Spreader' is easy to grow on most soils

GARDENING WITH **SHRUBS**

ABOVE *Ilex aquifolium* 'Aurea Maculata' is distinctive with gold centres to the leaves

Shrubs noted for their fragrant flowers

Buddleja (many)
Chionanthus virginicus
Choisya 'Aztec Pearl'
Daphne (many)
Lonicea (many)
Mahonia japonica
Osmanthus
Philadelphus
Rosa (many)
Skimmia japonica
Syringa (many)
Viburnum (many)

Shrubs for sandy soil

Berberis
Ceratostigma
Cistus
Convolvulus
Continus
Cotoneaster
Cytisus
Genista
Helianthemum
Hibiscus
Lavatera
Ozothamnus
Perovskia
Potentilla
Rosmarinus
Spiraea
Ulex

Shrubs for shade

Aucuba japonica
Camellia
Fatsia japonica
Hypericum calycinum
Ilex aquifolium
Ligustrum (most)
Lonicera
Rubus
Skimmia
Viburnum davidii
Vinca

ABOVE **'Dorothy Perkins'** – an old favourite rambling rose

GARDENING WITH **SHRUBS**

Shrubs for chalky soils

Aucuba
Berberis
Buddleja
Ceanothus (some)
Chaenomeles
Choisya
Cistus
Deutzia
Escallonia
Forsythia
Fuchsia
Garrya
Hypericum
Ilex
Kerria
Lavandula
Ligustrum
Mahonia
Olearia
Paeonia
Philadelphus
Pittosporum
Potentilla
Prunus
Pyracantha
Ribes
Rosmarinus
Santolina
Senecio
Syringa
Weigela
Yucca

ABOVE LEFT **Paeonia rockii requires a humus-rich, well-drained soil**

LEFT **Prunus sargentii has bronze-red leaves and pink flowers**

HANDY GUIDES

Shrubs for clay soils

Aucuba
Berberis
Chaenomeles
Choisya ternata
Cornus
Cotoneaster
Forsythia
Genista
Hypericum
Philadelphus
Potentilla
Pyracantha
Ribes
Rosa
Spiraea
Viburnum
Weigela

Shrubs that require well-drained acid soils

Calluna
Camellia
Cassiope
Corylopsis
Crinodendron
Daboecia
Erica (summer flowering)
Hamamelis
Kalmia
Pernettya
Pieris
Rhododendron
Skimmia
Vaccinium

ABOVE LEFT The bridal wreath (*Spiraea arguta*) – masses of small white flowers in spring

LEFT *Pieris japonica* 'Dorothy Wyckoff' is a popular US-raised variety

CHAPTER NINE

GLOSSARY

LEFT Rosa 'Trumpeter' is one of the best floribundas

GARDENING WITH **SHRUBS**

ABOVE *Ribes roseum* 'White Icicle'

ABOVE *Rosa* 'Charles de Mills'

acid soil A soil that contains no free lime, with a pH value of less than 6.5

AGM The Award of Garden Merit – an award given to plants that have exceptionally good garden qualities, presented by the Royal Horticultural Society

alkaline Soils where lime is present

basal A shoot emerging from the neck or crown of a plant

blotched Petals with irregularly scattered colour patches

boss Prominent centre stamens

cold frame An unheated box with sides of wood, plastic or brick, and which has a removable transparent top, used to protect plants from the cold

crown Area of plant from which shoots and roots grow

cuttings Pieces of shrubs, removed and rooted to form new stock

cultivar Cultivated variety

dead heading Removal of dead flowers

deciduous Loses leaves in winter

die-back Death of a plant's tissue, beginning at the tips and slowly travelling along the stem

division Dividing a plant; a form of propagation

evergreen Retains foliage throughout the winter

fungicide Product to treat fungal diseases such as mildew and rust

ground cover Low-growing shrubs or plants

grow on Leave to grow until of a size suitable for planting out

humus Organic matter in soil

hybrid Plants raised from two species, varieties or cultivars

insecticide Chemical product used to control insect pests

layering Pinning a piece of plant onto the ground, where it will

GLOSSARY

develop roots and grow; a form of propagation

move on Transferring a plant to its permanent position

mulch Bulky organic matter applied around plants to conserve moisture and deter weed growth

nutrient deficiency Problems due to lack of essential elements in the soil

perennial Plants that grow and flower year after year

pH Measure of acidity

pinch out To remove, by hand, the growing tip of a plant

plant out To plant into a permanent, flowering position

prick out To remove seedlings from the pot or tray and space them into other trays to allow for an increase in size

propagator Item of equipment for raising seedlings or rooting cuttings

raceme Similar to a *spike* but with flowers on short stalks

reflexed Petals that are bent back

self-seeding A plant that scatters its seed naturally

stopping Taking out the growing tip to produce a more bushy plant

systemic Pesticide that is absorbed by the plant and travels through the plant in the sap flow

taken with a heel Cuttings taken to include a small portion of mature stem

tilth Fine soil in which to sow seeds

transplant Moving a plant from one place to another

umbel Type of flower head: umbrella-shaped

variegated Leaves that are blotched, spotted or edged with a different colour

virus Organism for which there is no cure, causing malformation and discoloration

woody Old, mature portions of stem

Mophead hydrangeas, with their large flower heads, are spectacular summer-flowering shrubs

Magnolia x *soulangeana* can grow tall – keep it in check by regular pruning

GARDENING WITH **SHRUBS**

ABOUT
THE AUTHOR

Plants have played an major part in Eric Sawford's life, even from before his school days – his father worked as a head gardener. At the tender age of 16 his sizeable and comprehensive collection of cushion-forming alpine saxifrages attracted the attention of the local newspaper, and were featured on the front page.

When Eric left school he worked for well-known nurserymen Wood & Ingram, until he was called up for National Service with the RAF. Back in civvy street he returned to gardening and although he continued working with plants, he also gained experience with seeds, garden machinery and other gardening products.

Over the years he has enjoyed growing numerous types of plants including shrubs, hardy perennials, bulbs, fuchsias and alpines (the latter to show standard, with more than a little success).

In the 1970s Eric began photographing plants and gardens. Wherever possible, he takes pictures of plants growing in their natural habitat, including alpines in the Alps and other subjects in warmer climates. As a result, he has built up an extensive photographic library; his fabulous pictures can be seen in numerous books, as well as the hundreds of features he has written for the national gardening press.

LEFT *Chaenomeles* 'Crimson & Gold'

INDEX

Pages highlighted in **bold** include illustrations of plants

A
Abelia 17
    grandiflora 15
Abeliophyllum 11
Acer 55
    palmatum 'Dissectum' **54–55**
acid soil 5, 21, **63**, **78**, 155
alkaline soil 5, 21
andromeda 121
aphids 47
apothecary rose 1
Aucuba 56, 154, 155
    japonica 153
        'Variegata' **33**, 56
autumn-flowering shrubs 17
azalea **6**, **47**
Azara 57
    serrata 57

B
'balled' shrubs 22, 27
barberry 59
'bare-root' shrubs 3, **4**, 21–22, **25**, 27
basal cuttings 39
Berberis 13, 59, 153, 154, 155
    x *media* 'Red Jewel' **58–59**
    x *stenophylla* 'Corallina Compacta' **20–21**
birds 49
blackfly 47
box 61
Brachyglottis 'Sunshine' **143**
bridal wreath 155
broom 83, 93
Buddleja 3, 13, 60, 153, 154
    davidii **60**
bush rose 134–135

butterfly bush 3, 60
Buxus 61

C
cabbage tree 75
calico bush 106
Californian lilac 67
Calluna 17, 63, 155
    'H.E. Beale' **62–63**
    vulgaris 15
Camellia 21, 47, 65, 153, 155
    'Adolphe Audusson' **36–37**
    'J.C. Williams' **64–65**
    japonica 11
    x *williamsii* 17
    'Taylor's Perfection' **48**
canker 49
capsid bugs 49
Cassiope 155
caterpillars 49
Ceanothus 15, 67, 154
    griseus var *horizontalis* **66–67**
Ceratostigma 68, 153
    plumbaginoides **68**
    willmottianum 15, 68
Chaenomeles 11, 69, 154, 155
    'Crimson & Gold' **69**
chafer beetles 49
chalky soil 5, 7, 154
cherry 49
Chilean lantern tree 82
Chionanthus virginicus 153
chlorosis 50
Choisya 70, 154
    'Aztec Pearl' **44–45**, 153
    ternata 13, 155

INDEX

'Sundance' **70**
Cistus 13, 43, 71, 153, 154
    purpureus **42**, **71**
clay soil 155
Clematis 13, 47, 73
    alpina 13, 73
    montana 'Elizabeth' **72–73**
    tangutica 73
container-grown shrubs 3, **4**, 21, 25, **26**
Convolvulus 74, 153
    cneorum 13, **74**
coral spot disease 50
Cordyline 75
    australis 'Torbay Red' **75**
Cornus 77, 155
    alba 'Aurea' **76–77**
        'Sirica' 5
    controversa 'Variegata' **10–11**
    mas 11
    stolonifera 'Flaviramea' 5
Corylopsis 6, 11, 78, 155
    sinensis **78**
Cotinus 79, 153
    coggyria **79**
Cotoneaster 13, 81, 153, 155
    conspicuus **80–81**
cotton lavender 142
Crinodendron 82, 155
    hookerianum 13, **82**
cuttings 39–41
Cytisus 13, 83, 153
    'Compact Crimson' **83**

D
Daboecia 155
daisy bush 114
Daphne 13, 84, 153
    cneorum 'Eximia' **22**
    × *kalmiiflora* **85**
    mezereum 11
        'Grandiflora' **84**
    odora 11
deadheading 31–32
deciduous shrubs 32–35

Deutzia 13, 85, 154
diseases 49–50
division 41
dogwood 77
dwarf box 61

E
English rose 135
Erica 15, 17, 87, 155
    arborea 'Albert's Gold' **86–87**
    carnea 6–7, 11
        'King George' 7
        'Springwood White' 7
        'Vivelli' 7
    × *darleyensis* 6, 7, 11, 17
        'Darley Dale' 7
        'Molton Silver' 7
Escallonia 154
Euonymus 88
    'Emerald 'n' Gold' **88**
evergreen shrubs 22, 31, 35, **47**
Exochorda 89
    × *macrantha* 'The Bride' **89**

F
Fatsia japonica 153
feeding 35, 50
fireblight 49–50
firethorn 127
floribunda rose 135
foliar feeding 35, 50
Forsythia 11, 49, 90, 154, 155
    × *intermedia* 'Spectabilis' **90**
fragrant shrubs 153
French lavender **14–15**
Fuchsia 15, 17, 91
    magellanica 'Versicolor' **91**

G
Garrya 92, 154
    elliptica 11, **92**
Genista 13, **42**, 43, **93**, 153, 155

163

golden bell bush 90
greenfly 47

H
Halimium 94
    'Susan' **94**
Hamamelis 11, 95, 155
    japonica 11
    mollis 'Pagoda' **16–17**, 95
hardiness 5
hardwood cuttings **40**, 41
hardy plumbago 68
heather 6, **7**, 63, 87
Hebe 15, 17, 97
    'Caledonia' **96–97**
    ochracea 'James Stirling' **30–31**
heel cuttings 39, **40**
Helianthum 99, 153
    'Rhodanthe Carneum' **98–99**
Hibiscus 15, 17, 101, 153
    syriacus 15
        'Oiseau Bleu' **100–101**
holly 105
honey fungus 49
honeysuckle 111
hybrid tea rose 134–135
Hydrangea 15, 32, **102–103**, 159
    macrophylla **8–9**
Hypericum 15, **104**, 154, 155
    calycinum 153
    'Hidcote' 17

I
Ilex 105, 154
    aquifolium 153
        'Aurea Maculata' **152**
        'Silver Queen' **105**
iron 50

J
Japanese maple 55
japonica 69

Jasminum nudiflorum 11, 17
Jew's mallow 107

K
Kalmia 106, 155
    latifolia 13, **106**
Kerria 107, 154
    japonica 13, **107**

L
laurel 56
Lavandula 15, 108, 154
    angustifolia 'Rosea' **108**
    stoechas **14–15**
Lavatera 153
lavender 108
layering **41**
Ligustrum 109, 153, 154
    tschonoskii 'Vicaryi' **109**
lilac 49, **145**
Lonicera 111, 153
    fragrantissima 11
    nitida 'Baggeson's Gold' **110–11**

M
magnesium 50
Magnolia 113
    × *soulangeana* 13, **159**
    stellata 'Royal Star' **112–113**
Mahonia 11, 154
    'Charity' 11
    japonica 153
    × *media* 17
maple 55
Mexican orange blossom 70
mock orange 35, 119
mulching 31, **32**, 35

N
nematodes 47
nitrogen 50

INDEX

northern hemisphere 7
nutrient deficiencies 50

O
old rose 135–136
Olearia 114, 154
    cheesmanii **114**
ornamental bramble 139
ornamental cherry 125
ornamental currant 133
Osmanthus 115, 153
    × *burkwoodii* **115**
    delavayi 13
    heterophyllus 15

P
Paeonia 116, 154
    rockii **154**
    suffruticosa **116**
patio rose 136
pearl bush 89
Pernettya 155
Perovskia 15, 117, 153
    'Blue Haze' **117**
pests 47–49
Philadelphus 35, 119, 153, 154, 155
    'Belle Etoile' **118–119**
Photinia × *fraseri* 'Birmingham' **120**
Pieris 6, 21, 121, 155
    formosa **121**
    japonica
        'Dorothy Wyckoff' **155**
        'Valley Rose' **23**
Pittosporum 122, 154
    tenuifolium
        'Gold Star' **24**
        'Purpureum' **35**
        'Tom Thumb' **122**
planting 22, 25–26, **27**
potash 50
Potentilla 15, 123, 153, 154, 155
    fruticosa 'Limelight' **38–39**
    'Golden Spreader' **150–151**

    'Lemon & Lime' **123**
powdery mildew 50
pre-packed shrubs **4**, 4, 22, 27
privet 109
pruning 32–35
Prunus 49, 125, 154
    cerasifera 'Pissardii' **50–51**
    incisa 'Kojo-no-mai' **28–29**
    sargentii **154**
    tenella 'Fire Hill' **125**
Pyracantha 13, 127, 154, 155
    coccinea **126–127**
    'Orange Glow' **34**

R
red spider mites 49
Rhododendron 5, **6**, 13, 21, 22, 32, 47, 49, 129–130, 155
    'Bluebird' **18–19**
    'Crest' **130–131**
    'Gibraltar' **52–53**
    'Golden Flare' **2–3**
    'Irohayama' **46–47**
    luteum **12–13**
    'Morgenrot' **128–129**
Rhus 132
    typhina **132**
Ribes 11, 133, 154, 155
    laurifolium **133**
    roseum 'White Icicle' **158**
rock rose 71, 99
Rosa 134–137, 153, 155
    'Charles de Mills' **158**
    gallica officinalis 1
    'Madame Isaac Pereire' **134**
    rugosa 'Alba' **137**
rose 5, 49, 134–7, **153**, **156–157**
rose of Sharon 104
Rosmarinus 138, 153, 154
    officinalis 13
    officinalis 'Severn Sea' **138**
Rubus 139, 153
    biflorus **139**
    cockburnianus 5

'Golden Vale' **6**
Russian sage **117**

S
St John's wort 104
Salix 11, 141
    integra 'Hikuro-Nishiki' **26**
    lanata **140–141**
sandy soil 153
Santolina 142, 154
    pinnata **142**
screens 35
seasons 7
secateurs 35
seed 43
Senecio 143, 154
    greyi **143**
shade 153
shrubby bindweed 74
shrubby cinquefoil 123
shrubby mallow 101
shrubby veronica 97
silk tassel bush 92
Skimmia 13, 153, 155
    japonica 153
smoke bush 79
softwood cuttings 39
soil types 5, 21–25, 153–155
southern hemisphere 7
spindleberry 88
Spiraea 11, 13, 15, 144, 153, 155
    arguta **155**
    japonica 'Goldflame' **144**
spring-flower shrubs 13
stag's horn sumach **132**
stem-tip cutting **39**
suckers 41
sumach 132
summer-flowering shrubs 15
Sun rose 71
Syringa 13, 145, 153, 154
    vulgaris **145**

T
tea rose 134–135
tree peony 116

U
Ulex 153

V
Vaccinium 155
Viburnum 13, 147, 153, 155
    × *bodnantense* 11, 17
    carlesii **146–147**
    davidii 153
    tinus 11, 17
Vinca 153
vine weevils 47–49
virgin's bower 73
viruses 50

W
watering 32
wedding cake tree **11**
Weigela 13, 148, 154, 155
    'Florida Variegata' **148**
willow 49, 141
winter-flowering shrubs 11
witch hazel **16–17**, **95**
woolly aphids 49
woolly willow **140–141**

Y
Yucca 15, 149, 154
    gloriosa 15, **149**

Z
Zauschneria 15

TITLES AVAILABLE FROM
GMC PUBLICATIONS
Books

GARDENING

Alpine Gardening	Chris & Valerie Wheeler
Auriculas for Everyone: How to Grow and Show Perfect Plants	Mary Robinson
Beginners' Guide to Herb Gardening	Yvonne Cuthbertson
Beginners' Guide to Water Gardening	Graham Clarke
The Birdwatcher's Garden	Hazel & Pamela Johnson
Companions to Clematis: Growing Clematis with Other Plants	Marigold Badcock
Creating Contrast with Dark Plants	Freya Martin
Creating Small Habitats for Wildlife in your Garden	Josie Briggs
Exotics are Easy	GMC Publications
Gardening with Hebes	Chris & Valerie Wheeler
Gardening with Wild Plants	Julian Slatcher
Growing Cacti and Other Succulents in the Conservatory and Indoors	Shirley-Anne Bell
Growing Cacti and Other Succulents in the Garden	Shirley-Anne Bell
Growing Successful Orchids in the Greenhouse and Conservatory	Mark Isaac-Williams
Hardy Palms and Palm-Like Plants	Martyn Graham
Hardy Perennials: A Beginner's Guide	Eric Sawford
Hedges: Creating Screens and Edges	Averil Bedrich
Marginal Plants	Bernard Sleeman
Orchids are Easy: A Beginner's Guide to their Care and Cultivation	Tom Gilland
Plant Alert: A Garden Guide for Parents	Catherine Collins
Planting Plans for Your Garden	Jenny Shukman
Sink and Container Gardening Using Dwarf Hardy Plants	Chris & Valerie Wheeler
The Successful Conservatory and Growing Exotic Plants	Joan Phelan
Tropical Garden Style with Hardy Plants	Alan Hemsley
Water Garden Projects: From Groundwork to Planting	Roger Sweetinburgh

WOODCARVING

Beginning Woodcarving	GMC Publications
Carving Architectural Detail in Wood: The Classical Tradition	Frederick Wilbur
Carving Birds & Beasts	GMC Publications
Carving the Human Figure: Studies in Wood and Stone	Dick Onians
Carving Nature: Wildlife Studies in Wood	Frank Fox-Wilson
Carving on Turning	Chris Pye
Celtic Carved Lovespoons: 30 Patterns	Sharon Littley & Clive Griffin
Decorative Woodcarving (New Edition)	Jeremy Williams
Elements of Woodcarving	Chris Pye
Essential Woodcarving Techniques	Dick Onians
Lettercarving in Wood: A Practical Course	Chris Pye
Relief Carving in Wood: A Practical Introduction	Chris Pye
Woodcarving for Beginners	GMC Publications
Woodcarving Tools, Materials & Equipment (New Edition in 2 vols.)	Chris Pye

WOODTURNING

Bowl Turning Techniques Masterclass	Tony Boase
Chris Child's Projects for Woodturners	Chris Child
Contemporary Turned Wood: New Perspectives in a Rich Tradition	Ray Leier, Jan Peters & Kevin Wallace
Decorating Turned Wood: The Maker's Eye	Liz & Michael O'Donnell
Green Woodwork	Mike Abbott
Intermediate Woodturning Projects	GMC Publications
Keith Rowley's Woodturning Projects	Keith Rowley
Making Screw Threads in Wood	Fred Holder
Turned Boxes: 50 Designs	Chris Stott
Turning Green Wood	Michael O'Donnell
Turning Pens and Pencils	Kip Christensen & Rex Burningham
Woodturning: A Foundation Course (New Edition)	Keith Rowley
Woodturning: A Fresh Approach	Robert Chapman
Woodturning: An Individual Approach	Dave Regester
Woodturning: A Source Book of Shapes	John Hunnex
Woodturning Masterclass	Tony Boase
Woodturning Techniques	GMC Publications

WOODWORKING

Beginning Picture Marquetry	Lawrence Threadgold
Celtic Carved Lovespoons: 30 Patterns	Sharon Littley & Clive Griffin
Celtic Woodcraft	Glenda Bennett
Complete Woodfinishing (Revised Edition)	Ian Hosker
David Charlesworth's Furniture-Making Techniques	David Charlesworth
David Charlesworth's Furniture-Making Techniques – Volume 2	David Charlesworth
Furniture-Making Projects for the Wood Craftsman	GMC Publications
Furniture-Making Techniques for the Wood Craftsman	GMC Publications
Furniture Projects with the Router	Kevin Ley
Furniture Restoration (Practical Crafts)	Kevin Jan Bonner
Furniture Restoration: A Professional at Work	John Lloyd
Furniture Restoration and Repair for Beginners	Kevin Jan Bonner
Furniture Restoration Workshop	Kevin Jan Bonner
Green Woodwork	Mike Abbott
Intarsia: 30 Patterns for the Scrollsaw	John Everett
Kevin Ley's Furniture Projects	Kevin Ley
Making Chairs and Tables – Volume 2	GMC Publications
Making Classic English Furniture	Paul Richardson
Making Heirloom Boxes	Peter Lloyd
Making Screw Threads in Wood	Fred Holder
Making Woodwork Aids and Devices	Robert Wearing
Mastering the Router	Ron Fox
Pine Furniture Projects for the Home	Dave Mackenzie
Router Magic: Jigs, Fixtures and Tricks to Unleash your Router's Full Potential	Bill Hylton
Router Projects for the Home	GMC Publications
Router Tips & Techniques	Robert Wearing
Routing: A Workshop Handbook	Anthony Bailey
Routing for Beginners	Anthony Bailey
Sharpening: The Complete Guide	Jim Kingshott

Space-Saving Furniture Projects	Dave Mackenzie
Stickmaking: A Complete Course	Andrew Jones & Clive George
Stickmaking Handbook	Andrew Jones & Clive George
Storage Projects for the Router	GMC Publications
Veneering: A Complete Course	Ian Hosker
Veneering Handbook	Ian Hosker
Woodworking Techniques and Projects	Anthony Bailey
Woodworking with the Router: Professional Router Techniques any Woodworker can Use	Bill Hylton & Fred Matlack

CRAFTS

Bargello: A Fresh Approach to Florentine Embroidery	Brenda Day
Beginning Picture Marquetry	Lawrence Threadgold
Blackwork: A New Approach	Brenda Day
Celtic Cross Stitch Designs	Carol Phillipson
Celtic Knotwork Designs	Sheila Sturrock
Celtic Knotwork Handbook	Sheila Sturrock
Celtic Spirals and Other Designs	Sheila Sturrock
Complete Pyrography	Stephen Poole
Creating Made-to-Measure Knitwear: A Revolutionary Approach to Knitwear Design	Sylvia Wynn
Creative Backstitch	Helen Hall
The Creative Quilter: Techniques and Projects	Pauline Brown
Cross-Stitch Designs from China	Carol Phillipson
Cross-Stitch Floral Designs	Joanne Sanderson
Decoration on Fabric: A Sourcebook of Ideas	Pauline Brown
Decorative Beaded Purses	Enid Taylor
Designing and Making Cards	Glennis Gilruth
Glass Engraving Pattern Book	John Everett
Glass Painting	Emma Sedman
Handcrafted Rugs	Sandra Hardy
Hobby Ceramics: Techniques and Projects for Beginners	Patricia A. Waller
How to Arrange Flowers: A Japanese Approach to English Design	Taeko Marvelly
How to Make First-Class Cards	Debbie Brown
An Introduction to Crewel Embroidery	Mave Glenny
Making Decorative Screens	Amanda Howes
Making Fabergé-Style Eggs	Denise Hopper
Making Fairies and Fantastical Creatures	Julie Sharp
Making Hand-Sewn Boxes: Techniques and Projects	Jackie Woolsey
Making Mini Cards, Gift Tags & Invitations	Glennis Gilruth
Native American Bead Weaving	Lynne Garner
New Ideas for Crochet: Stylish Projects for the Home	Darsha Capaldi
Papercraft Projects for Special Occasions	Sine Chesterman
Patchwork for Beginners	Pauline Brown
Pyrography Designs	Norma Gregory
Rose Windows for Quilters	Angela Besley
Silk Painting for Beginners	Jill Clay
Sponge Painting	Ann Rooney
Stained Glass: Techniques and Projects	Mary Shanahan
Step-by-Step Pyrography Projects for the Solid Point Machine	Norma Gregory
Tassel Making for Beginners	Enid Taylor
Tatting Collage	Lindsay Rogers
Tatting Patterns	Lyn Morton
Temari: A Traditional Japanese Embroidery Technique	Margaret Ludlow
Trompe l'Oeil: Techniques and Projects	Jan Lee Johnson
Tudor Treasures to Embroider	Pamela Warner
Wax Art	Hazel Marsh

PHOTOGRAPHY

Close-Up on Insects	Robert Thompson
Double Vision	Chris Weston & Nigel Hicks
An Essential Guide to Bird Photography	Steve Young
Field Guide to Bird Photography	Steve Young
Field Guide to Landscape Photography	Peter Watson
How to Photograph Pets	Nick Ridley
In my Mind's Eye: Seeing in Black and White	Charlie Waite
Life in the Wild: A Photographer's Year	Andy Rouse
Light in the Landscape: A Photographer's Year	Peter Watson
Outdoor Photography Portfolio	GMC Publications
Photographing Fungi in the Field	George McCarthy
Photography for the Naturalist	Mark Lucock
Professional Landscape and Environmental Photography: From 35mm to Large Format	Mark Lucock
Rangefinder	Roger Hicks & Frances Schultz
Viewpoints from Outdoor Photography	GMC Publications
Where and How to Photograph Wildlife	Peter Evans

MAGAZINES

WOODTURNING ● **WOODCARVING** ● **FURNITURE & CABINETMAKING** ● **THE ROUTER** ● **NEW WOODWORKING**
THE DOLLS' HOUSE MAGAZINE ● **OUTDOOR PHOTOGRAPHY** ● **BLACK & WHITE PHOTOGRAPHY**
TRAVEL PHOTOGRAPHY ● **MACHINE KNITTING NEWS** ● **BUSINESSMATTERS**

The above represents a full list of all titles currently published or scheduled to be published.
All are available direct from the Publishers or through bookshops, newsagents and specialist retailers.
To place an order, or to obtain a complete catalogue, contact:

GMC Publications,
Castle Place, 166 High Street, Lewes, East Sussex BN7 1XU, United Kingdom
Tel: 01273 488005 Fax: 01273 402866
E-mail: pubs@thegmcgroup.com
Orders by credit card are accepted